AMERICA AS A PACIFIC POWER: CHALLENGES AND OPPORTUNITIES IN ASIA

HEARING

BEFORE THE

COMMITTEE ON FOREIGN AFFAIRS
HOUSE OF REPRESENTATIVES

ONE HUNDRED FOURTEENTH CONGRESS

SECOND SESSION

APRIL 28, 2016

Serial No. 114–202

Printed for the use of the Committee on Foreign Affairs

Available via the World Wide Web: http://www.foreignaffairs.house.gov/ or
http://www.gpo.gov/fdsys/

U.S. GOVERNMENT PUBLISHING OFFICE

99–949PDF   WASHINGTON : 2016

(II)

CONTENTS

Page

WITNESS

The Honorable Antony J. Blinken, Deputy Secretary of State, U.S. Depart-
ment of State 2

LETTERS, STATEMENTS, ETC., SUBMITTED FOR THE HEARING

The Honorable Antony J. Blinken: Prepared statement 6

APPENDIX

Hearing notice 48
Hearing minutes 49
The Honorable Edward R. Royce, a Representative in Congress from the
State of California, and chairman, Committee on Foreign Affairs: Material
submitted for the record 51
Written responses from the Honorable Antony J. Blinken to questions sub-
mitted for the record by:
The Honorable Ted Poe, a Representative in Congress from the State of
Texas 52
The Honorable Eliot L. Engel, a Representative in Congress from the State
of New York 58
The Honorable Matt Salmon, a Representative in Congress from the State
of Arizona 70

AMERICA AS A PACIFIC POWER: CHALLENGES AND OPPORTUNITIES IN ASIA

THURSDAY, APRIL 28, 2016

House of Representatives,
Committee on Foreign Affairs,
Washington, DC.

The committee met, pursuant to notice, at 10:08 a.m., in room 2172 Rayburn House Office Building, Hon. Edward Royce (chairman of the committee) presiding.

Chairman ROYCE. Committee will come to order.

Some of the world's most dangerous flash points are in Asia, as are some of our closest allies and these are critical relationships to foster. Deputy Secretary of State Blinken is just back from the region. We welcome him to the committee. America is a Pacific power, and we must act like one.

This committee has played a leading role in shaping U.S. policy toward Asia. We took the lead imposing tough sanctions on North Korea, on highlighting human rights in Southeast Asia, and in strengthening our alliances with democracies in the region.

Since North Korea's January nuclear test—its fourth—Kim Jung Un's belligerence has only increased. This rogue regime poses a direct threat to the United States. Last weekend the regime launched a missile from a submarine; reports suggest another nuclear test could be on the horizon. The good news is that earlier this year the President signed into law sanctions legislation this committee pushed to aggressively target North Korea's cash. This strong, bipartisan measure, authored by myself and Mr. Engel, helped the administration get a sweeping U.N. Security Council sanctions resolution through.

So the administration has the tools it needs to tackle the North Korean threat and keep Americans safe. But will it use them? A recent U.N. report found several countries still pushing cash to Kim Jung Un's regime through prohibited arms deals. They must be pressed to stop, forced to stop, and frankly, through this legislation we can force them. The administration must designate more companies, more banks, and more individuals. North Korea is a human rights house of horrors. So how is it that not one North Korean official has been sanctioned specifically for human rights abuses?

Looking south, the Beijing Government continues its aggressive push into the South China Sea with land reclamation and militarization of contested islands. Our allies are increasingly alarmed. And while these disputes must be resolved peacefully, that will be best done with a policy of strength, resolve, and clarity—rejecting Beijing's apparent moves toward de facto control over international shipping lanes.

In Southeast Asia, Vietnam's poor human rights record continues. Bloggers and journalists are harassed and jailed. When myself or other members of this committee—Chris Smith—when we have traveled to Vietnam we have visited with political prisoners. We have visited with dissidents. When the President travels to Vietnam next month, President Obama could send a clear and unequivocal message to the Communist government and firmly stand by that country's brave dissidents, unlike he did in Cuba. I would also urge the President to stress the importance of restoring the Bien Hoa Military Cemetery, the resting place of many South Vietnamese soldiers who fought to preserve their freedom, a cause especially important to the Vietnamese-American community.

And while there is hope for the new government in Burma, and we have been pushing for many years on this committee for democratization in Burma, it is making progress and it must now perform for all Burmese, including the Rohingya population. I hope to hear that we are making the protection of this persecuted minority one of our priorities.

Finally, no discussion of Asia is complete without mentioning its dynamic economies. We must continue efforts to open new markets for our businesses and build the capacity of tomorrow's trade partners. Trade can play a key role in strengthening U.S. alliances.

The United States has played a critical role in Asia. Our power and presence helped shape the economic miracles. When we think about what happened in Japan and in South Korea and in Taiwan, all vibrant democracies today, but that proud legacy has to be protected through constant vigilance and engagement.

Mr. Engel will be here momentarily. We'll move to introduce Mr. Blinken, we'll have your testimony and then we will hear from the ranking member when he arrives.

Thank you, Tony.

STATEMENT OF THE HONORABLE ANTONY J. BLINKEN, DEPUTY SECRETARY OF STATE, U.S. DEPARTMENT OF STATE

Mr. BLINKEN. Mr. Chairman, thank you very, very much and to members of the committee, thank you for having me here. It's very good to be back to discuss our rebalance to the Asia Pacific region.

I just got back from my sixth visit to the region in a little over a year and with each trip I have to tell you I've seen growing dividends of this effort to balance our focus on the region and to strengthen a rules-based, institutions-based order that is advancing our interests and increasingly not only in the region but globally.

Chairman ROYCE. Secretary Blinken, could you—could you pull the microphone just a little closer. Some of the members were having trouble hearing you.

Mr. BLINKEN. Sorry about that. Is that better?

Chairman ROYCE. Yes.

Mr. BLINKEN. Thank you.

Chairman ROYCE. Thank you, Tony.

Mr. BLINKEN. As you said, Mr. Chairman, really nowhere in the world are economic and strategic opportunities clearer or more compelling than in the Asia Pacific region, home to four of our top ten trading partners, five of our seven treaty allies, the world's largest and fastest-growing economies including 40 percent of overall global growth, nearly two-thirds of the global middle class and, of course, some of the most wired and innovative people in the world.

Over the last 7 years, this rebalance to Asia that is deepening our strategic, economic and diplomatic ties with the region commensurate with its importance has helped shape a positive trajectory in the region.

We have given substance to the rebalance by bolstering our treaty allies, deepening engagement with emerging powers, strengthening regional institutions, promoting trade and investment, enhancing our military posture, advancing democratic reform and creating new networks of trilateral and multilateral relationships.

There are multiple pillars to the rebalance. I just want to briefly go through—go through those pillars. First, we've invested in strengthening and modernizing our core alliances with Japan, with Korea, the Philippines, and Australia.

We've updated our guidelines for our defense cooperation with Japan, included new host nation support agreements with both Japan and Korea, signed a forced posture agreement with Australia, and included a landmark enhanced defense cooperation agreement with the Philippines.

Second, we've deepened engagement with emerging countries in the region. We've built a relationship with China defined by broader practical cooperation on global challenges while at the same time directly engaging our differences to try to resolve or narrow them while avoiding conflict. And we've worked to deepen the bonds between the people of the United States and Taiwan.

Our partnerships with Indonesia, Malaysia, and Singapore have grown to reflect our increased cooperation on regional and global challenges, everything from countering climate change to violent extremism and we've forged new relations with Vietnam and Burma as they start to turn the page on the past.

I just saw this again for myself in Vietnam last week. Thanks in part to the bipartisan leadership of this committee, the U.S. and Vietnam are deepening and broadening our ties in areas that we couldn't even imagine a decade ago, even a few years ago, from military cooperation to human rights to peacekeeping.

Third, we sustained an increased engagement with the institutions of the region like the East Asia Summit, APEC, ASEAN, including by sending our first dedicated Ambassador to ASEAN, hosting the first ever U.S.-ASEAN summit here in the United States, and hosting APEC in 2011.

These are important forums for promoting collective action and facilitating the peaceful resolution of differences. They advance a regional economic, political, and security architecture in which the United States is a vital and permanent player.

Fourth, we have vigorously promoted trade and investment opportunities designed to unlock growth for the United States as well as for our allies and partners in the region. We've implemented a free trade agreement with South Korea. We've worked with Burma to modernize and strengthen legal and regulatory regimes, helping set the stage for major American companies to enter that market.

And, of course, the heart of our engagement in the region economically is the Trans-Pacific Partnership, which will bring 12 APEC economies and 40 percent of global GDP together. TPP will eliminate more than 18,000 taxes on American exports and help level the playing field for American workers while solidifying an economic arena in which every participant, regardless of its size, agrees to fight bribery and corruption, abide by international labor standards including the formation of independent trade unions, and commits to enforcement of environmental safeguards.

Fifth, we've enhanced our military posture in the Asia Pacific, deploying nearly 60 percent of our Navy in the region by the end of the decade and some of our most advanced capabilities. We are increasing the maritime security capacity of our partners and we are rotating American personnel into new and more places like northern Australia and new sites in the Philippines.

Sixth, we are standing up for our values, for the basic rights and freedoms of individuals throughout the region. In Indonesia and the Philippines we are working with our partners to tackle corruption and strengthen institutions. And then, of course, in support of Burma's historic elections and peaceful transition of power, we helped establish the nation's first nonpartisan independent election observation organization. We trained over 11,000 political party members to improve their ability to effectively communicate with voters. We continue to stress the importance of upholding the rule of law and express our strong concern about discrimination experienced by ethnic and religious minorities including the Rohingya.

In response to our engagement and demands from the Vietnamese people, Vietnam has taken some positive steps on human rights including releasing political prisoners, ratifying the Convention Against Torture and the U.N. Convention on the Rights of Persons with Disabilities, and agreeing to allow independent trade unions for the first time in modern history. Significant reforms remain to bring Vietnam's domestic laws into sync with international human rights obligations and, indeed, with its own constitution.

Seventh, and finally, we've invested in a new geometry of trilateral and multilateral networks to encourage cooperation among and between countries in the region. At the core of these efforts is a very robust trilateral partnership with South Korea and Japan, under which we convened the first ever trilateral meeting at the vice minister or deputy level. I've now done that three times, and the benefits of this relationship are crystal clear in the face of the region's most acute challenge—the challenge from North Korea and its provocative acts in the nuclear missile domain. We are stepping up trilateral cooperation on sanctions implementation, including under the new U.N. Security Council resolution.

We are working trilaterally to increase the capabilities of other countries to implement that resolution and our three countries will continue to shine an intense light on North Korea's deplorable human rights violations and pursue accountability for them.

We are also intensely focused on maritime issues, especially China's assertive and provocative behavior in the South China Sea that is challenging respect for international law, freedom of navigation, and the peaceful resolution of disputes.

We've also deepened our commitment to the U.S.-Australia-Japan trilateral strategic dialogue, hosted the inaugural of the U.S.-Japan-India trilateral ministerial dialogue.

These bilateral, trilateral, and multilateral relationships are not aimed at any particular country. They are not exclusive. We welcome any kind of flexible geometry of collaboration among countries that share important goals including steps toward greater China-Korea-Japan cooperation and the growing unity of the ASEAN community.

And we are building interconnected relationships not just among countries but among people. The YSEALI community, now 67,000 strong, connects dynamic young people throughout the region to the United States and to each other.

Mr. Chairman, these efforts represent a small but important slice of the work that we are currently undertaking. Seven years after President Obama rebalanced our sight on the Asia Pacific, we are leaders of a region increasingly bound by common ideals, shared prosperity, and a collective sense of global responsibility.

I thank you very much.

[The prepared statement of Mr. Blinken follows:]

DEPUTY SECRETARY BLINKEN
TESTIMONY
"AMERICA AS A PACIFIC POWER: CHALLENGES AND OPPORTUNITIES IN ASIA"
HOUSE FOREIGN AFFAIRS COMMITTEE
APRIL 28, 2016

Chairman Royce, Ranking Member Engel, Congressmen and Congresswomen – thank you, for the opportunity to come before you today to discuss a region whose importance will only grow in the years and decades ahead.

This past weekend, I returned from my sixth visit to the Asia-Pacific in a little over a year. With each trip, I have seen growing dividends of President Obama's rebalance to Asia and our common efforts with our Pacific partners and friends to strengthen a rules-based, institutions-based order that is advancing U.S. interests and addressing regional and, increasingly, global challenges.

Having inherited a nation immersed in the greatest financial crisis since the Great Depression, President Obama recognized from his first day in office that America's presence in the Asia-Pacific was not merely peripheral to our future prosperity and security—it was indispensable.

Nowhere in the world are our economic and strategic opportunities clearer or more compelling than in the Asia-Pacific—home to four of our top ten trading partners, five of the seven of our defense treaty alliances, the world's largest and fastest growing economies—including 40 percent of overall global growth and nearly two-thirds of the global middle class—and some of the most wired and innovative people in the world.

The rise of Asia will help define this new century. How it rises—according to which rules, by which means, to what ends—will have significant impact on our national well-being, perhaps more so than any other region in the world.

Over the last seven years, our rebalance to Asia—that is, deepening our strategic, economic, and diplomatic ties with the region commensurate with its importance—has helped shape and influence a positive trajectory. We've given substance to the rebalance by bolstering our treaty allies, deepening engagement with emerging powers, strengthening regional institutions, promoting trade and investment, enhancing our military posture, advancing democratic reforms, and creating new networks of trilateral and multilateral relationships.

As a result of our engagement, we are better prepared to meet the region's opportunities and to tackle its challenges, including concerns related to nuclear proliferation, intensifying maritime disputes, and backsliding in democratic governance and respect for human rights in some countries, in addition to global challenges like violent extremism and human trafficking.

First, we have invested in strengthening and modernizing our core alliances with Japan, South Korea, the Philippines, and Australia. Tested in crisis, fortified in peace, and bound by shared values, these relationships provide a foundation of peace and security in the region that has enabled decades of stability and prosperity.

For the first time in nearly two decades, we have updated our guidelines for our defense cooperation with Japan so that our forces will have the flexibility to face 21st century challenges. We have also concluded new host nation support agreements with both Japan and the Republic of Korea, reinforcing these alliances and underscoring our shared commitment to continuing U.S. presence in the region. We signed a Force Posture Agreement with Australia in 2014, and the first of 1,250 U.S. Marines on a six-month rotational deployment arrived in Darwin earlier this month. And we signed a landmark Enhanced Defense Cooperation Agreement with the Philippines to give our forces access to key facilities and allow our militaries to work even more closely together.

Second, we have deepened engagement with emerging powers and forged new relations with nations in the region as they start to turn the page on the past.

We have built a relationship with China defined by broader and deeper practical cooperation on global challenges and, at the same time, direct and frank discussions on areas of disagreement. Our engagement with China has helped it implement difficult reforms—including those that opened previously protected sectors of their economy to foreign competition—take steps to modernize its economy, and play a more constructive role in international efforts to tackle global challenges from Iran's nuclear program to North Korea's destabilizing nuclear and ballistic missile testing to progress against climate change including our work together on the recent Paris Agreement.

We are directly engaging on areas of difference with the goal to resolve or narrow them while preventing conflict. This is important, as significant areas of disagreement remain, including on issues concerning China's destabilizing behavior in the South China Sea, conduct in cyberspace, and its denial of internationally recognized human rights and fundamental freedoms to its citizens and those of other countries.

We have worked to deepen the bonds between the people of the United States and Taiwan. We continue to call on both sides of the Strait to engage in constructive dialogue on the basis of dignity and respect, which has laid the foundation for peace and stability across the Strait and led to a significant improvement in cross-strait relations. The United States remains committed to our one-China policy based on the three joint communiqués and the Taiwan Relations Act. We look forward to working with Taiwan's first female president and leaders from all parties to further strengthen our relationship.

For Indonesia, the biggest country and economy in Southeast Asia, we upgraded our relationship to Strategic Partnership to reflect our increased cooperation on global challenges such as countering climate change and violent extremism. Our Comprehensive Partnership with Malaysia is now two years old, and we have doubled the scope and scale of military cooperation, as well as signed two terrorist information-sharing agreements. Singapore continues to be a strong partner for the United States, as a member of the counter-ISIL coalition and a major commercial hub for more than 3,000 American companies. We recently upgraded our Enhanced Defense Cooperation Agreement with Singapore to expand our military relationship.

The recent elections and peaceful transition of power in Burma represent a historic milestone, and they offer a moment of opportunity for Burma to move forward with additional reforms to tackle the many challenges that still remain. The national reconciliation process must continue, the rights of ethnic and religious minorities must be respected, remaining political prisoners must be released, and broad-based economic growth must be sustained. We continue to work with the new government to offer any support we can to aid in Burma's success.

Thanks to leaders of both parties in the United States, the U.S. and Vietnam are deepening and broadening our ties in areas that we could not even imagine just a few years ago, including regional security, military cooperation, trade and business, human rights, climate change, global health, energy security, disaster response, and peacekeeping. In every one of those areas, our partnership is growing stronger every day.

Third, we have sustained and increased engagement with institutions of the region like the East Asia Summit, APEC, and ASEAN—including by sending our first dedicated Ambassador to ASEAN. Important forums for promoting collective action and facilitating the peaceful resolution of differences, these organizations advance a regional economic, political, and security architecture in which the United States is a vital and permanent player.

In February, President Obama became the first president to host the U.S.-ASEAN Summit in the United States, and we are proud to collaborate on a range of issues of global importance—from expanding economic integration through the ASEAN Economic Community to upholding international rules and norms in the maritime space..

We have also assumed a reinvigorated position in APEC—including by hosting in 2011—which allows use to promote a rules-based approach to the regional economic architecture. Recent successes include reducing tariffs on environmental goods and improving supply chain connectivity within APEC, as well as launching liberalization efforts for services and digital trade

Fourth, as a central pillar of our rebalance, we have vigorously promoted trade and investment opportunities designed to unlock growth for the United State and our allies and partners. We have implemented a free trade agreement with South Korea and worked with Burma to modernize and strengthen legal and regulatory regimes, helping set the stage for major U.S. companies like GE, Ford, Chevrolet, Coca-Cola, and Colgate-Palmolive to enter the market.

The heart of our economic engagement is the landmark Trans-Pacific Partnership, which will bring 12 APEC economies and 40 percent of the global together with the highest labor, environment, and intellectual property standards in the word.

TPP will solidify an economic arena where every participant—regardless of size—agrees to fight bribery and corruption, abide by international labor standards, including the formation of independent trade unions, and commits to enforcement of environmental safeguards.

It will eliminate more than 18,000 taxes on American exports and level the playing field for American workers. It will help allow for the free flow of ideas and data and promote additional standards that are critical for building the foundation of a common ASEAN digital economy. And it will mean simplifying the process to start a new business and streamlining ways to resolve business disputes.

American companies have been the largest source of foreign investment in ASEAN. As Secretary Kerry often points out, it is not only the quantity of these investments. It is their quality. American businesses help develop a skilled workforce, contribute towards responsible business conduct, and abide by the rules of the road.

Fifth, we have enhanced our military posture in the Asia-Pacific—deploying 60 percent of our Navy in the region by the end of the decade, including some of our most advanced capabilities. That includes F-22 and F-35 stealth fighter jets, P-8 Poseidon maritime surveillance aircraft, continuous deployments of B-2 and B-52 strategic bombers, and also our newest surface warfare ships, like the amphibious assault ship U.S.S America, and all three of our newest class of stealth destroyers, which will all be homeported with the Pacific fleet.

We do this in order to reinforce an environment of peace and stability that has provided value far greater than its cost. We are also bringing America's regional force posture into the 21st century by rotating American personnel into new and more places, like northern Australia and new sites in the Philippines and modernizing our existing footprint in Japan and the Republic of Korea.

We are increasing the maritime security capacity of our allies and partners to respond to threats in waters off their coasts and to provide maritime security more broadly across the region. We are helping the Philippines increase its naval and air forces, Vietnam expand its maritime domain awareness capacity, Malaysia improve its maritime law enforcement capability, and Indonesia protect its coastal communities and fisheries.

And we are holding more numerous and sophisticated exercises with a growing network of partner countries, none larger than this summer's RIMPAC, which will bring together more than two dozen navies—nearly twice the number that participated just six years and now including China—to increase our collective capacity for cooperation on humanitarian assistance and disaster relief operations.

The reason that we are the region's preferred security partner—the reason we are invited in and invited back—is not merely because of the professionalism of our armed forces. It is because, strong as we are, the United States accepts that the same rules apply to us as apply to all. We support the rule of law, even when it is not convenient.

Sixth, we have stood up for our values—for the basic rights and freedoms of individuals throughout the region. In January, the people of Taiwan showed the world again what a mature, Chinese-speaking democracy looks like. In 2014, Indonesia—a nation of 300 languages, 17,000 islands, and 250 million people—came together to hold the largest single-day election in the world and the most free, fair, and competitive presidential election in the history of Indonesia.

In Indonesia and the Philippines—both founding members of the Open Government Partnership—we are working with our partners to tackle persistent the challenge of corruption and strengthen the capabilities of their institutions.

In Burma, the United States is working in close partnership with the new government to support its efforts to fulfill the aspirations of its people. We supported Burma's first non-partisan, independent, election-observation organization, trained over 11,000 political party members from 84 political parties to improve their ability to effectively communicate with voters, and helped ensure that tangible benefits from the transition reach communities throughout the country.

Diversity is one of Burma's greatest strengths, and we continue to express our strong concern about discrimination and violent experienced by ethnic and religious minorities, including the Rohingya population in Rakhine State. Rule of law must be equally applied to ensure protection from violence, freedom of movement, access to livelihoods, education, and health, and an equal chance for everyone to participate in the democratic life of their country.

In response to our engagement and the demands from the Vietnamese people, Vietnam has taken positive steps on human rights, including ratifying the Convention against Torture and the UN Convention on the Rights of Persons with Disabilities, agreeing to allow independent trade unions for the first time in modern history, revising their civil code to make it easier for transgender persons to alter their legal identity and access health care, and broadening social media space as a way for citizens to share information and debate the issues of the day.

That said, citizens continue to be harassed or imprisoned for exercising their fundamental rights, and significant reforms must still be completed to bring Vietnam's domestic laws into synch with international human rights obligations and with Vietnam's own constitution. We continue to emphasize that our relationship can grow only as Vietnam demonstrates its commitment to human rights through concrete actions.

Thailand remains our most enduring Asia-Pacific partner in addressing a broad range of regional and global security, law enforcement, public health, and environmental challenges. In order to restore our relationship to its fullest capacity, however, we continue to encourage Thailand to return to civilian rule and restore full civil liberties to its citizens.

Seventh, we have invested in a new geometry of trilateral and multilateral networks to encourage cooperation among and between allies and partners.

At the core of these efforts, we have invested in a robust trilateral partnership with South Korea and Japan, two of our closest friends, partners, and allies. On the margins of the Nuclear Security Summit, the leaders of our three countries, President Obama, President Park, and Prime Minister Abe, met in Washington, DC to reaffirm a common vision for a rules-based order in the Asia-Pacific, where all countries act according to established laws and principles.

In support of these stronger ties, we have convened the first-ever trilateral meetings at the Vice Minister and Deputy-level, which have proved productive on a great range of issues. The benefits of our strong trilateral relationship are crystal clear in the face of the region's most acute threat: North Korea. We are expanding our cooperation even further in response to its provocative and destabilizing behavior. We are stepping up trilateral consultations on sanctions implementation, including those under UN Security Council Resolution 2270. We are working trilaterally to increase the capabilities of others to counter North Korean proliferation activities. And our three countries will continue to shine an intense light on North Korea's deplorable human rights violations and pursue accountability for them.

At the same time, our commitment to the Republic of Korea's security is absolute. We have begun consultations on the possible deployment of THAAD, which would provide additional defensive capabilities to protect South Koreans and the tens of thousands of U.S. personnel and their families on the peninsula.

With every trilateral meeting, we increasingly magnify the impact of our trilateral partnership beyond the immediate region. Since January, we have had separate trilateral meetings of cyber and health experts, including discussing our support for cyber capacity building and our collaboration against deadly epidemics, like Zika and Ebola. We are also teaming up in the fight to cure cancer, an effort at the center of the White House's Cancer Moonshot Initiative, led by Vice President Biden.

This summer, we will convene our first trilateral Middle East dialogue in Washington to discuss a common approach to key issues—from countering Daesh to fighting violent extremism to alleviating suffering and providing humanitarian assistance in Iraq and Syria.

We will also participate in a trilateral women's empowerment meeting in July in Washington that will invite civil society and business to the table.

At Japan's invitation, our trilateral development experts will also meet to coordinate our initiatives in the Lower Mekong and beyond, as well as put together a humanitarian assistance and disaster response working group to test our collective readiness on a range of natural disaster scenarios.

Our three nations are intensely focused on maritime issues, especially China's assertive and provocative behavior in the South China Sea that is challenging the principles of international law and the peaceful settlements of disputes, freedom of navigation, overflight, and other lawful uses of the sea, and unimpeded lawful commerce. Our security and prosperity depend on upholding these principles.

Taken together, these outcomes show that the statecraft of our leaders has paved the way for an early harvest of renewed trilateral cooperation on many of the world's most important issues.

We have also deepened our commitment to the U.S.-Australia-Japan Trilateral Strategic Dialogue, a model engagement for the region since it was first established in 2002. Senior officials and working groups meet regularly to coordinate defense, non-proliferation, security assistance, and development policies. President Obama and his Australian and Japanese counterparts held a Trilateral Strategic Dialogue meeting in November 2014.

Last year, Secretary Kerry hosted the inaugural U.S.-Japan-India Trilateral Ministerial dialogue, where our three countries agreed to work together to maintain maritime security through greater collaboration, as the U.S. and India welcomed Japan's participation in the 2015 MALABAR exercise.

Our bilateral, trilateral, and multilateral relationships are not aimed at any particular country. They are not exclusive. We welcome any kind of flexible geometry of collaboration among countries that share important goals, including steps toward greater China-Korea-Japan cooperation and the growing unity of the ASEAN community.

We are building interconnected relationships not just among countries but also people. Under the leadership of President Obama, we have expanded educational and exchange networks—creating the YSEALI community, now 67,000 strong, to connect dynamic young people throughout ASEAN to the United States and to each other. One of the highlights for President Obama, Secretary Kerry, and myself as we travel throughout the region is spending time with these young people. I have been deeply impressed by their sophistication, ingenuity, and global perspective.

CONCLUSION

We intend to continue our leadership on each and every one of those efforts, but in order to fully seize the opportunities at hand, we need to make sure that our efforts are resourced in accordance with our interests. Sustained U.S. commitment, not just through words but resources, is essential to help build a more mature security and economic architecture to promote stability and prosperity.

I am grateful to this Committee's Asia subcommittee for hosting Assistant Secretary Russel last week to discuss the President's $1.5 billion FY 2017 budget request for East Asia and the Pacific.

FY 2017's budget provides additional diplomatic, public diplomacy, consular, development and security assistance resources needed to unlock significant strategic and economic opportunities for the United States in this dynamic region. This funding allows us to maintain a strong presence as a preeminent trade and investment partner, security guarantor, and supporter of democracy, human rights, and good governance throughout the region.

Mr. Chairman, this all represents a small but important slice of the efforts we are currently undertaking from Seoul to Sydney. This record highlights just some of these key relationships as examples of what we have accomplished and what more is possible in the coming years.

Our intensive engagement in Asia has helped foster an increasingly broadly accepted vision for the future of the region, and for our role in it. A vision wherein countries come to each other's aid in times of disaster or crisis. Where borders are respected and countries cooperate to prevent small disputes from growing larger. Where disagreements are settled openly, peacefully, and in accordance with the rule of law. Where diversification of trade and investment flows allow countries to pursue their interests freely. And where the human rights of each and every person are fully respected.

This is our vision for the future of the Asia-Pacific, one of increased freedom, opportunity, and prosperity for all.

Thank you for the opportunity to speak with you today and I look forward to taking your questions.

_____

Chairman ROYCE. Thank you, Mr. Blinken.

I think without objection the witness' full prepared statement will be made part of the record and members are going to have 5 calendar days to submit statements and questions and extraneous materials for the record.

I think what we'll do is proceed with some of the questions from the committee and then when the ranking member arrives he'll make his statement and ask the Deputy Secretary of State the questions that he has as well.

If we could start, Mr. Blinken, with the North Korea sanctions and the administration of those sanctions, an issue I brought up in the opening statement. This is a strong North Korean sanctions bill that we passed and this bill did help get that U.S. resolution in place. But you're just back from the region.

What has been the reaction to this new law? How has the pressure been turned up? I raised the fact that no one has been sanctioned yet on human rights. I think it is high time that happened. And I know there's a new U.N. report that points out that several countries are still purchasing North Korean weapons. If you would speak to that issue. European luxury goods are still making their way to Kim Jung Un and are we yet to hit any Chinese banks facilitating transactions as we did in the past with Banco Delta Asia which was, frankly, very effective at the time, if you'll recall. It cut off the hard currency, stopped the production of the missile program at the time because they didn't have the hard currency to proceed.

Mr. BLINKEN. Thank you, Mr. Chairman.

First, I want to thank the committee for the very important work that it did. I think the combination of the U.N. Security Council resolution, which is the strongest tool we've had to deal with North Korea, the legislation from Congress, and the Executive order that have put those into effect really puts us in a different position.

We now have the ability if implemented—and that is the key—to maximize pressure on North Korea to try to get it to change its conduct. For the first time through the U.N. Security Council resolution we require that all cargo going in and out of the country be inspected. For the first time we have sectoral sanctions that limit or in some cases ban the export of critical materials—coal, iron, gold, rare earth materials that are what they use to finance their activities. And we have financial sanctions that go at banks and assets and we also have a ban on all dual-use nuclear and missile-related goods.

The critical component now is implementation and we are looking principally at China as well as other countries to follow through on implementation. China played an important role in getting the Security Council resolution. It is our expectation that it will now implement it. It's too soon to say whether that is the case. We've seen some encouraging developments including regulations that its promulgated, statements that it's made but we are now watching intensely.

But at the same time, it is not enough, and what we are focused on besides the implementation of the Security Council resolution is relentlessly building pressure on North Korea, working principally with our key allies Japan and Korea.

We are working in various ways to cut off all the revenues going to the regime. For example, they have, as you know, overseas workers whose remittances are not going back to their families but are going to the regime. We are working to cut those off. We have so-called diplomats engaged in illicit activities procurement but also even in illicit businesses that were the restaurant workers who defected from China. We are seeing this in different countries around the world. They set up businesses and the money goes back to the regime. We are working relentlessly to find those places and to get countries to cut them off. We are working to further isolate North Korea by getting their diplomats who are, again, not engaged in diplomatic activities sent home.

We are making sure that people don't go out to North Korea including for the Worker's Party Congress or invite them to international events and we are working as well to get countries to make sure that they're doing exactly what you alluded to—making sure that the ships that go to North Korea don't dock in their countries and that the planes don't land.

So right now we are working on enforcing all of that.

Chairman ROYCE. And I have been part of the dialogue—our committee has on each of these fronts and all have been helpful but there is one final step that needs to be taken. Banks are concerned about the reputational risk of what will happen if they have to make a choice between doing business with North Korea or doing business with the United States, and we've seen in the past for those dozen banks that were affected back during the sanctions regime put in place when North Korea was caught counterfeiting our $100 bills.

Just how concerned they are about reputational risk, even when—even when those sanctions were reported listed by State at the time Banco Delta Asia still wanted to know yes, but has the U.S. Treasury Department really signed off on this because otherwise we are not going to move the hard currency into North Korea.

Without that hard currency, they find it very difficult to move forward with their nuclear program and their missile programs. So it is essential that decision be made and we are going to continue to dialogue on that. But that is a decision you need to make and I am sure you raised that in Beijing.

Mr. BLINKEN. Appreciate that.

Chairman ROYCE. The last two—again, I'd raise that issue about the Rohingya people. We'll need to be working with that new government, frankly, in Burma to shape attitudes toward the Rohingya and you're going to have to continue to lean in on that.

On the Vietnam human rights issue, I've just got to share with you—we've got the case of a human rights—Nguyen Van Dai, who was arrested in December for his advocacy of human rights and advocacy of democracy. According to his wife, he was severely beaten by the police. He's been in solitary confinement since his arrest. He was denied access to his lawyers and to his family. Will the President push for his release? I think this is very, very necessary.

Mr. BLINKEN. Mr. Chairman, I very much appreciate those comments. First, on the Rohingya, we have been very focused on working the get the government in Burma to protect their rights. When I was there most recently a couple of months ago I raised this repeatedly including with Aung San Suu Kyi. We are looking to the government to give them genuine freedom of movement so that they can work, so that they can go to school, so they can get health care, and the discrimination. We are working on that.

With Vietnam, absolutely. I think the President will certainly engage with that community. When I was there last week, I met with civil society activists and lawyers and others, indeed, to express the concern that we have.

Vietnam has made real progress, as you know. They released a lot of political prisoners. They're working to conform their laws to the constitution. But work remains to be done.

Chairman ROYCE. Thank you, Deputy Secretary Tony Blinken. I appreciate it. We'll now go to our ranking member, Mr. Eliot Engel from New York, who has an opening statement first to make and then he'll have question.

Mr. Engel.

Mr. ENGEL. Well, thank you. Thank you very much, Mr. Chairman. Thank you for calling the hearing and Mr. Deputy Secretary, I've known you a long time. Welcome to the Foreign Affairs Committee.

It's been a pleasure working with you over the years in the various roles in which you've served and we are very fortunate to— I want to say this publicly—we are very fortunate to have such a dedicated and capable person as the number two in the State Department. So thank you for all you do.

I was encouraged that the President and Secretary Kerry charged you with focusing on Asia during your time as Deputy Secretary—that is a focus we badly need—and I think you're the right person for the job.

Half the world's population calls Asia home and the nations of Asia now account for more than a third of global GDP. From India to Japan, from Indonesia to Micronesia, Asia has a greater impact on global affairs than ever before.

As a Pacific power, the United States faces no shortage of foreign policy challenges in Asia, from North Korea's reckless behavior, to the impacts of climate change, to the recruitment of fighters into violent extremist groups.

The way we manage the rise of China in the years ahead may well be the most consequential foreign policy issue of the 21st century. The decisions we make today will determine whether the value and the norms we championed in Asia after World War II will continue to thrive.

That's why this has been called this America's Pacific century and that is why there is no better time to focus on this dynamic part of the world.

The so-called Asia rebalance has hatched a number of important diplomatic achievements. We've strengthened our core regional alliance with Australia, Japan, Philippines and South Korea.

With our ally Japan we've established new trilateral forums with Australia, South Korea and India. We've ramped up our engagement with ASEAN and demonstrated a clear commitment to the East Asia Summit, and we have normalized relations with Burma as that country has emerged from decades of isolation and begun the hard work of moving toward a more open democratic society.

Yet, despite all these efforts, I regularly hear concerns from our allies and partners in the region that the rebalance is more a shift in military strategy than about diplomatic engagement.

So this morning I hope we can drill down and look at other ways the State Department is making Asia a priority in areas in where the department's approach could be more robust.

I'll start with a question that sounds more like it should be on a geography quiz. As far as the State Department is concerned with respect to the Asia rebalance, what do we consider to be Asia?

I ask this because in my view the world's largest democracy, India, should be an integral part of our Asia policy. As the world's third largest economy, India has the potential to become a major economic player in East Asia and is already playing a constructive role in maritime issues.

China regards Asia as a strategic hole with its One Belt, One Road policy aiming to expand Chinese influence beyond East Asia through Central Asia to the Caspian.

Yet, the State Department structure with three different bureaus responsible for South and Central Asia and East Asia and the Pacific I believe creates an artificial barrier to cooperation across the entire region.

So I would like to hear about what the State Department is doing to overcome obstacles and deal with Asia as a whole single strategic priority that includes South and Central Asia.

Staying for a moment with structural issues at the State Department, I'd like to discuss if we are doing all we can from a resource standpoint to ensure our Asia policy will succeed.

The East Asia bureau is the smallest regional bureau in terms of personnel and the region accounts for the second lowest level of foreign assistance. Now, obviously any questions about State Department resources has to start here on Capitol Hill.

I strongly support investing more in diplomacy and development across the board. Our international affairs budget gives us tremendous bang for the buck. But I also wonder whether anything can be done in Foggy Bottom so that the rebalance is adequately resourced.

We've heard again and again that this is a priority and that should be reflected in the investments we are willing to make.

Lastly, I'd like to turn to the South China Sea. We expect the Law of the Sea Tribunal to issue a decision in the next month or so involving the claims of China and the Philippines. China's response to the ruling could ratchet up tensions.

While the United States doesn't take a position on the specific claims made by various parties, we do want to see China play by the same rules as everyone else.

So I support the ideas behind the Pentagon's Southeast Asia Maritime Security Initiative which aims to help our Southeast Asian partners know what China is doing off their coastlines and to share that information with each other.

If the U.S. and our partners are on the same page we can work together to keep China in check and make sure China doesn't threaten our strategic and economic interests in the region.

But it is not clear to me why the Defense Department is leading the way on this instead of the State Department. DoD's new authorities for this program are entirely duplicative of existing State Department authority.

I worry that putting such a program under DoD's control could erode State security cooperation responsibilities. Our diplomats are responsible for overseeing security assistance and it should stay that way, and whatever level of cooperation exists between State and DoD on this matter, I am concerned that this is another example of what some call the militarization of foreign policy. This feeds into those concerns that the Asia rebalance is a military policy even in areas that have traditionally been diplomatic responsibilities.

So, Mr. Deputy Secretary, I am interested in hearing your views on these issues as well as some other areas I'll be touching on as well. I thank you again for your service and commitment. I look forward to your testimony.

I want to raise two questions in conjunction with my statement and it is—the first one's about India. It's been characterized by U.S. officials as an indispensable partner of the United States.

As I mentioned before, it is the third largest economy in the world by purchasing power parity and is the largest democracy in the Asia region. The U.S.-India relationship is important. It's growing in particular on the defense side and Prime Minister Modi will be coming to Washington again in a couple of months to meet with President Obama.

From a strategic perspective, India is a potential counterweight to China's growing regional influence in Asia. They've become increasingly vocal on issues like freedom of navigation in the South China Sea and Indian Ocean region.

Additionally, Central Asia occupies critical geography in Asia sandwiched between China, Russia and Iran. The Chinese recognize this potential of Central Asia for what has been historically a strategic crossroads at the doorstep of the great powers and a transit point for trade and culture between the East and the West, and the Chinese are aggressively seeking to expand their influence there.

Yet, in your written testimony there's only one mention of India in the context of a U.S.-Japan-India trilateral ministerial and there are no other mentions of South or

Central Asia at all.

So my question is does South and Central Asia not fit with the administration's larger rebalance to Asia strategy and how can we be rebalancing to Asia without a strategic framework that considers Asia as a strategic whole?

Thank you.

Mr. BLINKEN. Thank you very much.

We strongly share your view on the importance of India both in and of itself but also as part of the region and as an increasingly vital regional actor.

India has its own regional policy that dovetails very nicely with the work we are doing on the rebalance. So we are working increasingly to integrate India into these efforts and you mentioned the one thing that I did point to in the statement—I think there may be more in the written statement—this U.S.-Japan-India trilateral effort at a ministerial level. Also we included Japan in the

Malabar exercise, which was a significant development which we hope to continue to carry forward.

But we are doing two things. We are building our own relationship with India as evidenced by the extraordinary level of high-level engagement, including Prime Minister Modi's return visit here, the President being received for the first time as the honored guest at Republic Day but also in very concrete collaboration across the board, everything from climate and Smart Cities to improving the business climate to defense cooperation to production cooperation even in the defense area. But intelligence sharing, information sharing, counterterrorism, countering violent extremism—across the board the relationship has been elevated.

But critical to this is exactly what you're pointing to, which is integrating India into these regional frameworks so that we are working together jointly and, again, the example with Japan is a very good. But this is exactly the direction that we want to go in.

Mr. ENGEL. Thank you.

I am wondering if you could comment on the South China Sea. I just want to ask you, the Philippines has brought an arbitration case against China's claims in the South China Sea under the United Nations Convention on the Law of the Sea.

If the ruling goes in the Philippines' favors it is expected, and if China refuses to abide by it what are the implications for the Philippines and other claimants in the South China Sea, and how would this change the U.S. approach in the South China Sea?

Mr. BLINKEN. Thank you.

Well, first I'd say this is—South China Sea is incredibly important to us and to all of our partners in two ways.

First of all, 25 percent of all traded goods, 25 percent of all that travels by sea goes through the South China Sea and, indeed, one-third overall of liquefied natural gas.

We have no position, as you know, on the sovereignty claims. We are not a claimant ourselves. But we have a very strong interest in the way these claims are prosecuted by an claimant and a very strong interest in maintaining freedom of navigation, in making sure that disputes are resolved peacefully and the countries abide by international law and these are the very interests that China has been challenging with some of its actions, including the massive reclamations and militarization of these land features as well as various assertions that are not justified under international law.

The case that you refer to is a very important moment. This is an arbitration case brought by the Philippines with China and we expect a decision by the tribunal in the coming months.

China knowingly agreed to the provisions in the Law of the Sea Treaty when it signed up. Five independent arbitrators said—unanimously rejected China's claim that it wasn't bound by the arbitration mechanism—that the jurisdiction was lacking.

And the convention provides that its rulings are binding on the parties to the convention. So we have worked very hard to establish across the region an understanding that this is appropriate mechanism—arbitration to resolve these disputes and that the ruling of the tribunal should be binding on the two parties.

We said to the Chinese, if you're given satisfaction on any aspect of the decision we'll be the first to stand up and defend it. But, of course, if the Philippines is you'll have to respect that.

China has a decision to make depending on how the ruling comes out. It will either decide to abide by the ruling and that gives us a great opportunity, I think, to narrow the scope of areas that are in dispute in the South China Sea. That would be good to get countries to work cooperatively together, for example, joint ventures on the exploitation of resources and to then work to resolve their disputes that remain peacefully. That's one path.

The other path is it ignores the decision, and then I think it risks doing terrible damage to its reputation, further alienating countries in the region and pushing them closer to the United States.

China will have to decide depending on what the results of the arbitration are. We are watching that very, very closely.

Mr. ENGEL. Thank you.

Chairman ROYCE. We go to Ileana Ros-Lehtinen of Florida, our chairman emeritus.

Ms. ROS-LEHTINEN. Thank you so much, Mr. Chairman. Thank you to the ranking member.

Secretary Blinken, for over a month I have been trying to get a hold of you by phone to discuss the problem between Morocco and Ban Ki-moon. You've not had the courtesy to return my call.

But at a hearing 10 days ago, Secretary Anne Patterson promised to work with me and the members of our Middle East Subcommittee regarding the draft U.N. resolution that would renew the mandate of MINURSO.

It was obvious that this was going to be a problem for weeks and I would have appreciated a call back. As you know, the draft in its current form could very well jeopardize our relationship with Morocco and our important military and intelligence cooperation.

There's got to be a way that we can find a compromise here and we can do it without including the controversial provisions, including the one that will allow Ban Ki-moon yet another opportunity to insult Morocco and do further damage. So I strongly urge you to work with the Moroccans today and to fix it.

What can you tell us about the draft resolution and what progress have we made?

Mr. BLINKEN. Thank you.

First, let me—let me apologize to you if I didn't get back to you. I am sorry about that. I'd be very happy to follow up immediately this afternoon——

Ms. ROS-LEHTINEN. Thank you, sir.

Mr. BLINKEN [continuing]. If that is convenient to you. So I am very sorry about that.

Ms. ROS-LEHTINEN. That would be great. Thank you, sir.

Mr. BLINKEN. Second, with regard to the situation, we've been deeply engaged in this since this problem first emerged and that was the Secretary General's visit to the region.

We worked very closely with Morocco and the U.N. to see if we could de-escalate the problem and get them working together. I immediately saw the foreign minister from Morocco. I was on the phone with him immediately. He came to visit me in my Office. Secretary Kerry saw him. We've had calls to—to the king.

Here's where we are. Morocco was very concerned with some of the things the Secretary General said during his visit to the region. We worked to ask the Secretary General to clarify what he meant and he did that.

We said to our Moroccan friends that we hope that as we were looking at renewing the MINURSO mandate we wanted to renew it for 1 year without any changes. Unfortunately, one of the things that Morocco did in response to the Secretary General's visit is they unilaterally decided to reduce and ask for the removal of members of the MINURSO mission.

That creates a problem for us because as a member of the Security Council we also have an important stake in making sure that U.N. peacekeeping missions' integrity is upheld and if we allow a precedent by which a country can unilaterally decide whether to accept or shut down a mission or change its composition that is going to be a real problem potentially in other areas with countries that, unlike Morocco, are not close friends or partners.

Ms. ROS-LEHTINEN. But when the Secretary General of the U.N., sir, makes such a provocative statement and accusation against Morocco it really pinned them against the wall.

Mr. BLINKEN. And I think that is exactly why we worked with the Secretary General's office to get a clarification of what he meant and what he didn't mean.

Our hope is that we can now get this resolution to a place where Morocco's concerns are answered but also the integrity of the peacekeeping missions are upheld and that it can go back to fully functioning as it was before.

That's what we are trying to achieve. But I want to assure you we share your commitment to the relationship with Morocco. This is one of our closest partners in the region and indeed around the world.

Ms. ROS-LEHTINEN. It sure is. We need more Morocco.

Mr. BLINKEN. So I thank you—I thank you for that.

Ms. ROS-LEHTINEN. And moving on. Thank you, sir.

At a hearing of the Middle East and North Africa Subcommittee, GAO testified that the State Department is not in compliance with the Iran, North Korea and Syria Nonproliferation Act, or INKSNA, a law that I authored several years ago.

INKSNA is an important nonproliferation tool. GAO told us that State's noncompliance has probably undermined the credibility of our sanctions.

We learned that State took almost 3 years to prepare one report and then implement sanctions and that your predecessor sat on the report for more than a year as it awaited approval.

So given that precedent, do you have an INKSNA report that you're sitting on and have you signed off on it and what's the status of that report, sir?

Mr. BLINKEN. I believe the next report is being actively worked on and processed. It has not come to me yet. I can assure you that as soon as it does I will move it out of my inbox as quickly as possible.

Ms. ROS-LEHTINEN. Thank you so much. Thank you, Mr. Chairman.

Chairman ROYCE. Thank you, Ileana.

We go now to Mr. Brad Sherman of California.

Mr. SHERMAN. Mr. Blinken, congratulations on the new position. It's good to hear that you'll have a policy of returning members' phone calls and I hope that doesn't just apply to the lady from Florida.

Asia's important. That's why it's important that we not enter into bad trade deals or unnecessary military confrontations in Asia.

Now, anyone who questions the adventures that are planned is patted on the head and told, well, you just don't understand how important Asia is.

No, Asia is so important that we better think carefully about our policy. When it comes to trade, we are given straw men. We are told well, if you don't like TPP then we could have no trade, or we could continue the unbalanced trading system that we have now without every discussion about a radical departure from our current trade system designed to achieve balance trade.

And when we are told that maybe we shouldn't be seeking a new cold war over some islets, we are told that 25 percent of the world's trade goes through the South China Sea. The vast majority of that goes in or out of Chinese ports, meaning that if China had military control of these islets that may actually belong to them anyway, they would be able to blockade their own ports. I don't think that is something we have to spend a lot of money preventing.

There is a tendency when making policy to yield to the interests of the most powerful entity in this country that cares about that policy, and that is why when it comes to trade policy, Wall Street is in the driver's seat.

But the deal is so bad that it has to be sold as a China containment policy because it is certainly not a jobs creation policy. But China enshrines the standard that currency manipulation goes hand and hand with trade deals. So they're the big winner. But they're even a bigger winner in the roles of origin where goods that are admitted to be 60 percent made in China and actually it'd be 95 percent made in China can then get a polish in Japan or a few parts added in Vietnam and be fast tracked into the United States.

So when it comes to the geopolitics, the Pentagon is very powerful in crafting American national security policy. What meets their needs now is a worthy uniformed adversary. Every time our military has gone up against a ragtag uniformed adversary it has been an unpleasant experience since the Philippines insurrection. Every time we have gone up against a uniformed foe it has been a relatively glorious experience, the most glorious perhaps winning the Cold War without a major confrontation with the Soviet Union.

So it is not surprising that these islets which are not ours, that do not have oil, and if there were any oil it would belong to the people unwilling to spend their own money to defend these islands—that these are exaggerated into great importance.

I am not saying that we don't care about navigation, we don't carry about—it obviously important. But to reconfigure the entire Pentagon to spend the lion's share of a $600 billion defense budget on confronting China, and you can't—it is a tough cost accounting job to determine what the defense budget is being spent on geographically.

But is—but I want to go to a completely different question: North Korea. North Korea needs about 12 nuclear weapons to defend themselves from us. They have about 12 nuclear weapons. They're creating enough fissile material for another two or three weapons a year. They need money. Iran now has—we can argue about it—$50 billion or $100 billion burning a hole in their pocket. North Korea sold the technology for the Al-Kibar Syrian-Iranian nuclear weapons program that the Israelis bombed in 2007.

Is the administration working toward an understanding with China that a Iranian plane will not be allowed to fly to North Korea without stopping in China for fuel? And please don't tell me we intercept ships. Please don't tell me that North Korean planes might not be allowed to do this. I am talking about an Iranian plane going nonstop to Pyongyang and coming back with a bomb.

Mr. BLINKEN. Thank you.

First, let me just say before addressing the question, which I very much appreciate, with regard to South China Sea, we are not looking for conflict.

We are looking to prevent conflict and what's at stake here is not just the transit of energy, oil and goods, as important as that is. There are larger principles at stake and these principles go to the entire foundation of the international order. If we don't defend those principles everywhere where they're being challenged the entire order that we invested so much in building over 70 years is at risk. That's why this is a big challenge.

Mr. SHERMAN. Mr. Blinken, I'll agree with you. But at the same time, if an Argentine plane was getting too close to the Falkland Islands we wouldn't be talking about it here.

Mr. BLINKEN. You know, we engage with the freedom of navigation operations around the world, not just in the South China Sea. Most of them are actually——

Mr. SHERMAN. I know. This one is getting a lot more attention.

Mr. BLINKEN. But leaving that aside, with regard to Iran and North Korea, this is something we are watching very carefully and you're right to, I think, raise the subject.

They've had a history of political engagement. Some of the reports of military, missile, nuclear engagement have been much harder to verify. What we are doing——

Mr. SHERMAN. Mr. Blinken, are you denying the reports that the Al-Kibar nuclear——

Mr. BLINKEN. No, no. I am saying——

Mr. SHERMAN [continuing]. Arms facility was North Korean technology?

Mr. BLINKEN. I am just saying that what we are looking at is the concrete evidence of relationships across the board, beyond the political.

What we are focused on is exactly what you pointed to. I think you make a very important point. What we are trying to do with regard to North Korea is to make sure that not only can its ships not dock but its planes. Air Koryo cannot land, not just in Iran but——

Mr. SHERMAN. Mr. Blinken, my question was about an Iranian plane flying to North Korea.

Mr. BLINKEN. And we are working to make sure under these——

Mr. SHERMAN. Are we working to get China to say that they won't allow the plane to go across China without stopping for fuel where it could be inspected? That is the only question.

Mr. BLINKEN. All of——

Mr. SHERMAN. You're free to address others but that is the only question.

Mr. BLINKEN. All of the members of the United Nations are bound by the Security Council Resolutions that say that there should be no military ballistic missile or nuclear cooperation with the DPRK.

As a result, they have——

Mr. SHERMAN. So the Iranian plane would—if it went to North Korea would be violating the U.N. resolution but if it flew nonstop over China no one would know about it. So you're relying on Iran's dedication to adhering to U.N. resolutions?

Mr. BLINKEN. We are looking to every country involved to make that on its——

Mr. SHERMAN. I would urge you to talk to Beijing about making that plane land because if your sole defense for what I laid out is that the Iranians wouldn't want to violate a U.N. resolution and they'd feel bad about violating international law, that is insufficient defense.

If the Iranian plane going to North Korea does not stop in China then it may not have a trade delegation on it. It may have cash going one way and nuclear weapons going the other way and that is a very specific issue.

I yield back.

Chairman ROYCE. To the point that Mr. Sherman is raising, without objection I am going to put in the record a U.N. document that is drawn from some of our Treasury documents that show two suspected primary arms dealers from North Korea who visited the Islamic Republic of Iran and that information, because it goes to the point that was being made by the gentleman of California.

Thank you, Mr. Blinken.

We may be—we may have follow-up questions from the members on this specific issue.

We now go to Mr. Chris Smith of New Jersey.

Mr. SMITH. Thank you very much, Mr. Chairman, and thank you, Mr. Blinken, for your presence here today.

The wire service writers did an extremely disturbing expose last year—a series of investigative reports—that found that the Obama administration gave undeserved passing grades to 14 countries with deplorable, and in many cases, worsening sex and labor trafficking records including China and Malaysia in Asia, Cuba, Oman, and others, making up 14 countries.

I've had hearings on this. I actually did a hearing a few weeks ago that was titled "Get it Right This Time," with the new TIP Report that is poised to come out shortly, being very concerned that when the administration does what it did, and that is give undeserved passing grades to countries that have deplorable records. It sells out the trafficking victims in those countries and those who are hurt by those countries' governments and it also is a deplorable, I think, abandonment of human trafficking concerns that we as a nation have in a bipartisan way.

Will China's and Cuba's, for example, and the other records be whitewashed once again this year? Secondly, I met with Nguyen Van Dai in Hanoi in 2007. He is one of the greatest peaceful human rights lawyers that I have met and I have met many in dictatorships like Vietnam.

Will the President raise his case and demand his release? He has done nothing wrong, as you know, as we all know here in the United States, and he needs to be released immediately to let his wounds heal from the beatings that he has suffered at the hands of the Vietnamese Government.

Thirdly, India and Japan have engaged in, clearly, patterns of noncompliance with the Goldman Act on child abduction. I've had nine hearings on child abduction.

We've had parents, men and women, moms and dads, tearfully tell their stories with regards to Japan as well as India. And yet, they have not been leveled, especially Japan, having a pattern of noncompliance.

The April 30th deadline is fast approaching for that report. I hope that reality is contained in the report.

Finally, President Xi is on a tear, crushing civil society with his new draft law and crushing religious freedom, and even the churches—the Patriotic Church and the others that have worked in cooperation with the government are finding that their buildings are being demolished, their pastors are being incarcerated.

The G-20 will meet in Hangzhou in September. Our hope is that the President—and that is right where the crosses are being taken off churches, the bulldozing of churches is occurring—that the President will raise these.

The sinofication of religion by Xi Jinping, announced last year and just most recently in a speech he made, is all about all the religious bodies having no contact outside the country's borders, and secondly and ominously, that everybody of faith has to serve the Communist Party. That will destroy religion or at least it will attempt to do it. If you could answer this. Thank you.

Mr. BLINKEN. First, let me just express my own appreciation, the department's appreciation, for your personal leadership on these issues and the focus you brought to them. It makes a huge difference around the world and, indeed, I've heard in places I've gone that you've been there first and have been putting the spotlight on these issues and it really does make a huge difference.

With regard to trafficking in persons, I want to assure you we will do our very best to produce a gold standard report this year. We are working on it very hard. We've heard concerns that were expressed last year.

We've looked to makes sure that the process internally is as strong and effective as possible to produce the best possible report. People are working very hard on it and we hope that that is the conclusion you'll come to when you see it.

With regard to Vietnam, I was just there and indeed met with a number of civil society activists, lawyers. We raise both individual cases and systemic problems that are—that remain at Vietnam at the highest levels on a regular basis.

I can't talk to the President's schedule at this point but I am confident that he will be raising these issues. And I met with, I think, some of the same people that you've seen who are extraordinarily brave in what they're doing every single day.

With regard to parental/child abduction, I was also just in Japan and raised this with foreign minister, with the vice foreign minister, with other senior officials and we have concerns about Japan's implementation of their commitments under the Hague Convention and that is something that I know you've been very, very focused on. We are working on that.

Mr. SMITH. And would you yield briefly?

Also, those that were left behind from the date of ratification.

Mr. BLINKEN. Yes.

Mr. SMITH. Those cases are heartbreaking and multi-yeared.

Mr. BLINKEN. Yes, absolutely. We are focused on those as well as the cases that have arisen after the ratification.

And then with regard to China, we very much share the concern that you expressed. We see across the board a crackdown on human rights and civil liberties.

We've seen a crackdown against lawyers. I've met with a number of lawyers the last time I was in Beijing in January. I heard directly from them what that community is experiencing.

I've met with religious leaders as well and have heard what's happening there. The laws that you refer to, we've been very much engaged on them whether it is the NGO law, the cyber security law, the national security law, or the counterterrorism law and we have real concerns about the substance of the laws as well as the way they may be implemented.

The NGO law, as you know, they've moved the enforcement of that law to the Ministry of Public Security, which sends a terrible signal about how they see NGOs, which are actually acting to the benefit of China and its own people. So we share those concerns. I just want to assure you we will continue to put the focus on them and do what we can to make progress.

One aspect of this is not just us but us bringing together other countries to express concern because there is some strength in numbers. At the Human Rights Council in Geneva we got a dozen countries to sign a statement expressing their concerns about the evolution of human rights and civil liberties in China.

These things over time have an effect and, you know, we went through decades of Cold War with the Soviet Union. Members of Congress played leading roles in putting that spotlight on the Soviet Union and its human rights abuses. And for decades it didn't seem like anything was happening. There was no change, and then there was. So I think keeping at it as you are and as we are trying to do can make a difference. Thank you.

Chairman ROYCE. For that to happen the administration needs to change its position on our legislation—myself and Mr. Engel's overhaul of the Broadcasting Board of Governors with the same mission—that Radio Free Europe, Radio Liberty used to have during that period of time. We need to get back to broadcasting that information in to these countries where a totalitarian system prevents people from having free access, either on the Internet or radio or television, to the truth.

We go now to Mr. Gregory Meeks of New York.

Mr. MEEKS. Thank you, Mr. Chairman.

Thank you, Mr. Secretary. China's economy has entered a new phase. It has to contend with slower growth for the first time in decade and we should expect China to manage this shift with domestic and international actions that are nationalistic and even provocative. I am convinced that our reactions should be a deepening of our ties regionally and multilaterally. As we do, it is critical that we remember that some of our strongest partners in the Western Hemisphere are also strong partners in the Pacific realm and that we should build upon those relationships to work together in Asia.

And there is no question in my mind that economic and diplomatic engagement is our strongest means of influence globally and that certainly is the case in Asia. And I don't think militarily, when I consider any rise in tensions in the region as some do—I think about economic engagement instead, global rules and investment in cultural exchange.

In fact, oftentimes people are looking at it and they say China—well, I think TPP and the last I looked China is actually not a part of TPP. So when we talk about TPP and China a threat as we do TPP, well, TPP is actually a counter to China and hopefully will get China to then adhere to global standards and rules which they may not, which is more reason why we should do TPP because it is leveling the playing field for businesses with strong rules in place where they were weak or nonexistent.

But my question is from some of my colleagues that I, you know, hear issues back and forth as we debate this issue that even an agreement like TPP, that has high standards as you talked about, is only as good as its implementation and enforcement and that is what I keep getting back.

For example, I even have some concerns about governments that developed state-owned enterprises to avoid living up to their TPP commitments and localization requirements that limit the competitiveness of U.S. companies' all over dollar security.

So my question would be, first, how can the administration ensure that our TPP partners adhere to the rules of TPP, should we get it done, because that is always a question that some have. So how would we do that?

And secondly, you know, I think we do have to make the geopolitical—there is a geopolitical argument to be made. Geopolitically, what happens in the region that we are so concerned about if we don't do TPP?

Let me just ask those two questions first.

Mr. BLINKEN. Thank you very much, Congressman.

First, I think you're exactly right about the potential magnetic pull of TPP on countries that are outside of it including China. It so happened that I was in the region when the agreement was concluded and I was in Japan the day it was actually concluded. The Japanese were extremely excited because their own leadership had helped bring us to that point—Prime Minister Abe.

The next day I was in South Korea. The first question I heard I heard was when can we join. The day after that I was in Beijing and what I saw was quite striking.

They've done, if not a 180-degree turn at least a 90-degree turn including in state party media, saying oh, this is something that could benefit us because they don't want to be left behind.

But, of course, to get in they have to raise their game. They have to go to the high standards, not a race to the bottom. Environment, worker protections, intellectual property.

So this has the potential to pull countries up, not create a race to the bottom, including with China. Second, you asked very, I think, appropriately about enforcement, and Congressman Sherman brought up a very important point a moment ago some of the concerns we've had with past trade agreements including on rules of a region. I think that is a very well taken point. Unlike previous agreements, TPP actually includes a rule—a clear rule on rules of a region.

We want to make sure that parties that are not part of TPP can't go to another country, have a few things done and then have the product benefit from TPP's rules. So, for example, China finishing something in Vietnam—that is exactly why we insisted this rule be part of the effort.

But it has to be implemented and everything else has to be implemented. That's exactly why we've asked in our budget for a significant portion of resources to go to implementation. We want to make sure that it is done seriously.

Finally, I also agree very much with you that, look, we can debate the economic merits of TPP and no trade agreement is going to be perfect. I think that the larger challenge that we face is 95 percent of consumers live outside the United States. We have to reach them, and the question is how are we going to do that, under what rules, and who writes those rules? And I think we are always better off, even if imperfect, if we are the ones doing it as opposed to letting someone else do it. That's more likely to benefit our companies and workers with a level playing field and make sure that the standards are high, not low. But we can debate the economic merits of it.

Strategically, though, it sends a very important message. It sends to our partners in the region we are there to stay. It's not just a security issue that may come up and a challenge that may arise that gets our attention and then we lose our focus. We are tied to you economically as well as through security considerations. It has, again, this potentially magnetic pull on countries outside the agreement who want to join it to lift their standards. And it sets the standard for the values that we'd like to see throughout the region. If we don't have the agreement we jeopardize all of those interests.

Thank you.

Chairman ROYCE. We go to Mr. Dana Rohrabacher from California.

Mr. ROHRABACHER. Thank you very much.

Mr. Chairman, and I appreciate your leadership, Mr. Chairman, and the fact that you have spent considerable time and effort focusing on these specific issues.

And Mr. Secretary, I am a bit concerned maybe not about specifics as about as much as your admirable optimism. May be something that is admirable but it is also of concern to those of us who think things maybe are more serious than your optimism suggests.

Spratly Islands is not—I hope it can be taken care of in a consistent way is what you and Chairman Royce and others have tried to put forward as a game plan that would put them into a position or pressure the Chinese into a position that would not permit this type—what I consider to be aggression—aggression of the world order because you had no sovereignty over the Spratly Islands and now you have a claim by a dictatorial government in Beijing over a hunk of territory in the middle of the most important trading patterns in the world.

Japan and Korea are ultimate allies in that area—seem to be getting second shrift on this and I will have to say that this should be of great concern—a greater concern to us than I believe that the plan that is set would suggest because it is a pattern.

Spratly Island is not just taking—take on its own I would agree with a less aggressive approach to the Chinese. But instead, this is part of a very alarming pattern. The Chinese still make major land claims against India, for example.

I think their land claim against India is a big as Texas. You couple Spratly Islands with that, couple it with the fact that the Chinese are all over the world making deals with corrupt dictators in order to fence in the resources necessary for an industrial society, meaning cutting us off.

We have—we still have—basically for those of us who are—I think that the two-child policy still maintains the mass slaughter of innocent children in the womb and if not that—if you don't accept that about abortion at least you accept the fact it is a violation—an attack on women's rights to decide.

And, of course, you still have the Chinese brutally suppressing the Falun Gong and engaged in the murder of prisoners in the sale of organs.

So we are talking about a monstrous pattern here and the Spratly Islands should only be sort of the icing on the cake of how alarming this should be.

So I would hope that—and by the way, during this whole time that I am talking, while these patterns have been going on, we have permitted them to make a massive profit in their relationship with us economically. Now, again, you've made your case on the Pacific trade agreement.

It might give them some thought. But we are not withdrawing any of their ability to come here and make the profit they're already making.

And one last thought, and that is I think that we ought to be more concerned about Japan and South Korea, but especially Japan, than we are about trying to remain in a stable relationship with China.

And my question for you, while I still have a couple seconds left, and that is do we or do we not support President Abe's efforts to introduce him a new factor into the Pacific which might deter the Spratly Islands-type operation, meaning a rearming of Japan?

Do we support that? And, quite frankly, I think Japan has been our best friend through this entire Cold War, never faltering.

Maybe we should make sure we make it a more equal relationship with Japan and take Abe up on his answer.

Mr. BLINKEN. Thank you very much.

First, I'd like to just say with regard to optimism, I think it just may be an occupational hazard. But I appreciate the comment.

Two things—first, let me also raise—quickly say that the various aspects of China's policies that you refer to we share your view and object to them. It was an improvement to go from a one-child to a two-child policy. But we object to any limitations that a government would impose.

Second, we've called for the release of the more than 2,000 Falun Gong prisoners in Chinese jails as well as other people who are repressed for religious views as well as political views. The Chinese have said that they have stopped the organ harvesting policy of prisoners as of last year. We have to see if that is actually being implemented. But they have apparently made a change in that policy.

With regard to Japan and Korea, Congressman, we couldn't agree more. These countries—these two countries—are at the heart of everything we are doing in the region and I have to say from my experience at least not only over the last 7 years but particularly in this job over the last year where I've made four trips now to Japan and Korea, in my judgment at least the state of our alliances has never been stronger.

We have worked very hard in both countries to strengthen what we are doing with them. With Japan, we have a major achievement with the revision of the defense guidelines that are now allowing Japan, along with the changes that it is made in its own laws, to play a much more significant role militarily throughout the region.

This is something we worked very hard to achieve. It's going to allow us to expand our cooperation on everything from new realms like cyber and space but also intelligence surveillance and reconnaissance, missile defense, maritime security, logistics support, peacekeeping operations, humanitarian assistance—actually all of that as a result of this agreement.

We have a new host nation support agreement, as you know, where Japan is contributing significantly to the support of our forces there. And throughout the region we are working more closely than ever with them.

With the Koreans we have now an agreement that is conditions-based on the transition during wartime of operational control that we worked very hard on that.

We got another host nation support agreement from them for 5 years to support the presence of our forces there. We have a trilateral information-sharing agreement between us, Japan and Korea and I've worked very hard personally to build a trilateral cooperative relationship with us, the Japanese, and the Koreans because the three of us working together on these issues are a very significant and powerful force.

So we share the view that these two countries are at the heart of everything we are doing. Those two alliances are our most important and increasingly we are actually managing to work together.

Ms. ROS-LEHTINEN. Thank you so much. Thank you, Mr. Rohrabacher.

Mr. Sires of New Jersey.

Mr. SIRES. Thank you, Chairlady.

You know, I am from New Jersey and we are a big pharmaceutical state, and I am very concerned about what goes on with the intellectual properties in this part of the world. It's not just stealing technological and intellectual properties but it is also some of the biggest research companies that we have in our state are constantly complaining that we don't seem to do enough about stopping the stealing of our intellectual properties.

And now we have a couple of treaties coming up. I just want you to reassure me so when I go back and speak to these pharmaceutical companies that we are doing everything in our power to prevent this.

I mean, so can you ease my pain here?

Mr. BLINKEN. I hope so, Congressman. I do want to assure you this is an area of intense focus. It has been. It will continue to be for the duration of this administration. We have different agencies in the government that are intensely focused on this. We've made it a mission to both elevate intellectual property rights standards across the board, including through trade agreements like Trans-Pacific Partnership which would have the highest standards on intellectual property protections, as well as making sure that we enforce these protections.

With China as well, one of the things that we've spent a lot of time on is the deep concern we had with the use of the cyber realm to steal trade secrets and to use cyber for commercial gain. This is an issue that the President engaged directly with President Xi on and we got an agreement with the Chinese that they will not do that. Now, obviously, that has to be enforced and implemented. But we are looking at that very vigilantly.

At the same time, throughout the region and around the world we are trying to stand up every day for enforcing the intellectual property rights of our companies in every industry, including the pharmaceutical industry.

So this is very much at the top of the administration's agenda and I think when I hear my colleagues from Treasury, from Commerce, from USTR, they are intently focused on this.

So I do want to give you that assurance we are doing everything we can.

Mr. SIRES. Thank you.

And I know North Korea keeps invading our computers and our systems here. I was just wondering, are we reacting back or are we just trying to put up walls so they can't do it?

I mean, there's got to be a price to be paid for what they're doing.

Mr. BLINKEN. We've made clear that not only are we strengthening every possible defense but that we reserve the right to respond at a time and place of our choosing in a manner of our choosing so we are looking at a variety of ways of responding to any cyber provocation.

Mr. SIRES. You sound like Donald Trump. Thank you. I don't have any more questions.

Mr. CONNOLLY. Would my friend—are you——

Mr. SIRES. Yes, I'll yield to you.

Mr. CONNOLLY. I thank my friend.

Welcome, Mr. Blinken. I wanted to just follow up on my friend, Mr. Sherman's, statement against TPP and give you an opportunity.

So let's say we pull the plug on TPP. Either the administration says we give up, you're right, it is flawed, or we in Congress decide there's no way we are going to give this our approval ever. What happens in a region to which we are pivoting and where China has its hungry eyes on trade relationships and economic ties as well?

Mr. BLINKEN. Thank you, Congressman. I think a couple things happen.

One is that in the immediate we'll lose market share and the trade barriers that are high for our workers and our products will remain where they are and maybe they'll even get higher.

Second, we run the risk that other countries will try to take the mantle in writing the rules for how trade goes forward and I can almost guarantee you that if we are not the ones in the lead of that effort those rules will not be advantageous to our workers and to our companies and they certainly will not be advantageous to the standards. We want to set the highest possible standards when it comes to protecting labor, protecting the environment, protecting intellectual property, and good governance.

So I think we are at real jeopardy, potentially, if we don't go forward in seeing an environment turn against our interests when, to the contrary, this is an extraordinary opportunity.

Again, we have in the region, as people have pointed out, close to two-thirds of the global middle class by 2030. That has extraordinary potential as beyond what we see today as an export market for the United States.

Mr. CONNOLLY. Just one follow-up point. We hear lots of people rail against China and its trading practices and currency manipulation and so forth. For the record, do we have a free trade agreement with China?

Mr. BLINKEN. We are working on a bilateral investment——

Mr. CONNOLLY. Do we have a——

Mr. BLINKEN. We do not currently have a bilateral——

Mr. CONNOLLY. We do not have a free trade agreement with China?

Mr. BLINKEN. So no. But we are working on a bilateral——

Mr. CONNOLLY. But you can't blame free trade in the case of China, since we don't have a free trade agreement. Is that not correct?

Mr. BLINKEN. Well, I think it is—as you know—a very complicated picture over the last 30 or 40 years.

I think if you look at the displacement in manufacturing, for example, over the last four or five decades, and something that we are deeply concerned about because of the impact that it has on our fellow citizens, much of this, of course, predates any of the free trade agreements of the 1990s. This started, really, in the 1970s. Technology—robotics—is probably more responsible for those developments.

That said, it is vitally important that in the agreements we reach that the standards, particularly for protecting workers, are the highest possible and if the United States is not in the lead in forging those agreements those standards are not going to be the highest possible.

Mr. CONNOLLY. Thank you, and thank you, Ms. Chairman.

Ms. ROS-LEHTINEN. Thank you, Mr. Connolly, and I will move to Mr. Chabot of Ohio.

Mr. CHABOT. Thank you, Madame Chair.

Let me begin with Taiwan, Mr. Blinken. Taiwan is going to be swearing a new President in May. The DPP will be coming back into power.

Taiwan is, I believe, a very important U.S. ally and I would also expect the PRC in all likelihood to act up to try to throw its weight around. They are, after all, a classic bully. They want to show their displeasure, I think, in this election. They still have 1,600 missiles pointed at Taiwan. As Mr. Rohrabacher had mentioned, they're in the process of building islands, to the great dismay of all their neighbors.

They're militarizing those islands now, and this is all occurring at a time when this administration unfortunately is reducing or trying to reduce the size of our military, including our Navy, which I think is just a terrible idea.

We should, I think, clearly, first of all, make sure that Taiwan has a sufficient military and modernize that they are able to keep China from acting out.

I think the only way China reacts is if they think that Taiwan is weak and that the United States lacks the resolve to defend Taiwan.

What would you say on behalf of the administration to reassure Taiwan that the United States will have its back?

Mr. BLINKEN. Thank you very much, Congressman.

First, I think Taiwan has given the world a very vivid demonstration of what a democratic election is and what a democratic transition is.

Mr. CHABOT. I agree.

Mr. BLINKEN. That was a very powerful message.

Mr. CHABOT. Very good point. I agree.

Mr. BLINKEN. I met with the President—the new President. She came to visit Washington this past summer. We had a very good meeting with her at the State Department and we have strongly encouraged the Chinese to engage with her and with Taiwan in a manner of mutual respect, with flexibility to try to build on the positive developments in cross-strait relations over the last decade or so. We hope the Chinese will do that.

Second, we very much agree with you that what has given Taiwan the confidence to engage with mainland China is the support from the United States, including arms sales. We have wanted to make sure, as have previous administrations, that Taiwan could not be coerced into doing things against the will of its people. I think we've notified something like $14 billion in arms sales since 2010. We continue to look very actively at that. With regard to our own posture in the region, as I said earlier, we now have approaching 60 percent of our Navy in the region. We take very seriously that Taiwan must feel confident if it is to engage from a position of strength with the mainland.

The other thing I think is important, and I know you've been a strong advocate for this, is we want to make sure that Taiwan and the talents of it is people are able to be employed around the world against global challenges. And so part of that is making sure that Taiwan can be represented in international organizations and we've been working very hard on that, to make sure that in organizations where recognitions of state is not required they be allowed in as members and where it is that they be able to participate irrespective of whether their statehood is recognized.

So across the board we've been working to strengthen our ties to the people of Taiwan and support its efforts.

Mr. CHABOT. Okay. Thank you.

Let me turn to another topic. I don't know that we've discussed Bangladesh at any length this morning. I think they clearly deserve more attention than they often have received, either by this administration or just in a whole range of things. But, first of all, as we all know, an election was held a while back and Sheikh Hasina was reelected, of course. Khaleda Zia and her party boycotted the election and so the political situation is, I think, a bit iffy there.

But let me ask you this. Bangladesh has long been considered a moderate Muslim country and resisting Islamic radicalism. There have been a couple of incidences just within the last week where we've seen a gay activist who was murdered. We've seen an English university professor publicly murdered and it is believed that these are linked to extremist Islamic intolerant type groups. Could you comment on that and what could be done about it?

Mr. BLINKEN. Yes. I am glad that you're putting the focus on that because that is a concern that we very much share. We've seen a series of terrorist attacks in Bangladesh over the last several months including the ones that you referred to, which Daesh or al-Qaeda have taken credit for.

Now, the government has sometimes claimed that these attacks were actually the work of the opposition in one fashion or another. But what we've seen, based on the evidence to date, is in fact that extremist groups, whether they are indigenous or whether they really are affiliated with ISIL or Daesh, are responsible and this gives us concern about the potential for ISIL, for Daesh, to take root in Bangladesh which, as you rightly pointed out, has been an important country in terms of a Muslim majority country with a moderate orientation that can be an important player in dealing with the problem of violent extremism.

So as a result of that, we have been both engaging with the government on this problem but also, for example, with India, given the relationship between India and Bangladesh, to raise the concern and to try to work together with them on countering violent extremism before it takes root in Bangladesh. That's the last thing we want.

Mr. CHABOT. Thank you.

Ms. ROS-LEHTINEN. Thank you, Mr. Chabot.

And now we'll turn to my good friend, Mr. Deutch of Florida.

Mr. DEUTCH. Thank you, Madam Chairman.

Deputy Secretary Blinken, thanks for being here today. Thanks for you service to our country and thanks for always being accessible to this committee. We appreciate it very much.

I would like to get back to talking about China. There's been a lot of discussion this morning about trade. I'd actually like to shift to foreign direct investment and in particular two areas: The area of security and the area of reciprocity.

Through One Belt, One Road, and the Asian Infrastructure Investment Bank, China has demonstrated a significant interest and willingness to invest abroad both in private and public capacity. But the domestic ownership requirements in China and some security review that takes place I referred to, I think, as an opaque security review, in China continues to frustrate American investors there. So I'd just like to know, as they pursue more outlets for foreign investment, what are our options for encouraging reciprocity? Why don't you answer that first and then I'll get to the security issue.

Mr. BLINKEN. Thank you.

Two things on that, Congressman.

First, with regard to their investments abroad, just on the first part of that equation, as a matter of principle, investments particularly in infrastructure in various parts of the world—Africa, Latin America, Central Asia, you name it—are welcome and needed.

But what has concerned us with regard to China is that those investments be made to high standards, not low standards, and again, worker rights, environment, intellectual property, good governance.

So they've established the Asia Infrastructure Investment Bank. We are not a part of that, although if the bank now operates to those high standards we'd welcome finding ways to work with it and other existing institutions.

But the key is those standards, and what I think we found with China investing abroad is that sometimes the bloom comes off the rose after a while because what tends to happen is this is usually commodities driven. They're trying to get commodities out of the countries that they're investing in. They do invest in infrastructure. They put a lot of money in. They have a lot more state money than we have to invest. But typically they import hundreds of Chinese workers to actually build the projects, as you know, and that doesn't sit well necessarily with the host governments.

The quality of what's built may not be up to standards and that tends to turn things a little bit so I think they have to look at that a bit carefully.

When it comes to our own investment and ability to invest in China, we are working across the board to get much greater access to get rid of some of the restrictions that inhibit our ability to do this.

This is very much part of our agenda with them and part of the bilateral investment treaty that we are seeking to negotiate is focused on exactly that.

Mr. DEUTCH. Great. Then on the—and particularly on the issue of Chinese direct investment in the United States, the Committee on Foreign Investment in the U.S.—CFIUS—has turned down a number of high-profile Chinese acquisitions on national security grounds.

Other deals fell apart and they were abandoned in anticipation of difficulties with CFIUS. But CFIUS only reviews a small number of transactions every year and I have two questions.

One, how might CFIUS alter their approach if there is a bilateral investment treaty with China and I guess the bigger question is with the really significant amounts of capital that the Chinese are looking to invest in the United States, does the CFIUS process still work?

Is it sufficient, given what might be coming, to safeguard our national economic security interests, the cyber interests—all of the sorts of things that we've been discussing already here today. Does this creation that has been around since the mid-70s still work or should we be looking at this in a new light?

Mr. BLINKEN. I think it is an excellent question and one that deserves a lot of thought. I think the first point that you made is important. The CFIUS only winds up applying to a very, very small percentage of the investments that are made or sought to be made. So we are talking about a pretty narrow universe to begin with.

Second, as a matter of principle, we welcome investment. This is good for our companies. It's good for all sorts of industries and it is something that as a general proposition we want to encourage. But it is vitally important that when it comes to national security we remain vigilant and that is what CFIUS is designed to do.

Now, I think you're right to raise the question about whether in the event of a bilateral investment treaty the investment flow goes up significantly, is that going to put further strain on the process and do we need to look at it. That's something I'd like to come back to if I can because it is a very good question that I need to think through a little bit more.

Mr. DEUTCH. Great. I would welcome that and happy to discuss that further with you, too. Thank you very much. Thanks, Madam Chair.

Ms. ROS-LEHTINEN. Thank you, Mr. Deutch.

Mr. Poe of Texas.

Mr. POE. Thank you, Madam Chair. Thank you, sir, for being here.

I have a couple observations and I want to spend most of my time talking about China.

When I visited with Admiral Harris at Pacific Command I asked him this question—of these five entities—Russia, China, North Korea, ISIS, and Iran—I think those are threats to the United States—which of those five do you think is the most troubling at this point? And he responded North Korea. Would you agree with that assessment or not? I just need a yes or no.

Mr. BLINKEN. Yes.

Mr. POE. Okay. I want to talk about China. China—they have 1 billion more people than we do in the United States. I think some Americans don't realize how populated China is. And some facts about China—they are the number-one recipient of poached ivory from Africa. The elephants are dying off. They're being killed in Africa and the number-one recipient is China.

They are thieves. They steal our intellectual property. Cyber attacks—I believe they're responsible for those. They're bullying Asia, trying to make new sovereign territory in the South China Sea and then claim the area around it. They're helping Pakistan with intercontinental ballistic missiles.

And then you get to human rights—they're the worst offender I think in the world. They persecute Christians and other religious minorities and then they have this practice of putting people they don't like, like the Falun Gong, in prison and charging them with trumped up political crimes and then harvesting their body organs and selling those on the marketplace. That's probably the worst type of crime in the world, in my opinion.

And, of course, we don't say this anymore because it is not the right thing to say but they are still a Communist nation and I think that is who we are dealing with. And we talk about pivoting to China and whether they're a threat and what we are doing about it and you talked about how we are increasing and focusing militarily.

Let me just show you a few posters here. Here—I don't know if you can see this or not. I know you can't probably see that behind all this is China in the South China Sea and the Philippines. In 1999, this is the relative strength of China in the red and the United States in the blue. It's about equal.

Let's go to the year 2015. This is the Chinese buildup with ships, submarines, and planes and the United States' military strength in the area in 2015—I got this from Pacific Command—is about the same.

And Pacific Command expects that in 2020—if I can get the poster—it is going to look like this—that China will have all of these planes, intercontinental ballistic missiles, ships, submarines, and the United States' strength in the area is still going to be just about the same.

Without going into the details of how much of everything, do you agree that that is what is occurring in south China?

Mr. BLINKEN. Thank you, Congressman.

We've certainly seen a significant buildup in China's military capacity over the last couple of decades and in recent years.

Some of that, I guess, on one level is not surprising as China grows and is more engaged in the region. It wants to protect its expanding interests and what we've seen though are two things.

We've seen an investment in these new capabilities which I think the chart shows very well. Everything from cruise missiles, short and medium range ballistic missiles, high-performance planes, integrated air defense and, of course, the Navy.

They're investing in those capabilities. They're also engaged in trying to transform what had been a mass conscript ground-based force into a higher tech force as well.

Mr. POE. That's right. I don't even include the number of military soldiers and sailors and airmen in these poster.

Mr. BLINKEN. Yes.

Mr. POE. Let me——

Mr. BLINKEN. So but just to get to your, I think——

Mr. POE. So what is our response? That's my question.

Mr. BLINKEN. Two things. First, of course, their budget is opaque. It's hard to know exactly what they spend on the military.

Mr. POE. What is our response? I am limited on time. What's our response?

Mr. BLINKEN. So our response——

Mr. POE. This is taking place. What is the U.S. response to this, if anything? That's all I am asking you.

Mr. BLINKEN. Sure. A few things. First, our military budget remains roughly three times what theirs is and they're, of course, starting from a much lower base. So that buildup is significant but they're trying to match something that is started at a much higher level and continues to invest at a significantly higher level. Second——

Mr. POE. But this is our presence in the area over here.

Mr. BLINKEN. It'll be about 60 percent of our Navy by 2020. Our technological capabilities, our experience, our capacity remains greater by far than any nation on earth including China and, again, I would defer to my military colleagues. I don't believe that is going to be challenged anytime soon.

Mr. POE. So you're saying that even though this is our presence in the area—the theater, I think, is the word—that it really doesn't alarm you because we are building up our capacity in the future?

Mr. BLINKEN. No, I would say that we are being very vigilant about the growth in China's military capacity. We are making sure across the board when it comes to any country that our own country remains unmatched.

Mr. POE. Okay. If I may have one question, and go back to North Korea, the biggest threat supposedly in the area. North Korean intercontinental ballistic missile capability—they're developing the concept not land to land—not sending something from North Korea over to Texas—their idea is build submarines and put intercontinental ballistic missiles on the subs and then float them around the Pacific and be the threat that we are. Is that a fair statement of what the North Koreans are trying to do?

Mr. BLINKEN. Yes, that is part of their strategy.

Mr. POE. All right. Thank you, Madam Chair. I appreciate getting this time.

Ms. ROS-LEHTINEN. Thank you, Mr. Poe.

Mr. Cicilline of Rhode Island.

Mr. CICILLINE. Thank you, Madam Chair. Thank you, Mr. Secretary, for your service and for being here today.

I want to turn again to the issue of China and after President Obama and President Xi met in Washington on the 31st of March, the two leaders affirmed cyber commitments that were announced in September 2015 and agreed to ensure their full implementation. Five days after that, Admiral Rogers, the commander of the U.S. Cyber Command, testified to Congress that, and I quote, "Cyber operations from China are still targeting and exploiting the U.S. Government, defense industry, academic and private computer networks."

So my first question is, are you aware of cases in which the Chinese Government may have supported cyber-enabled theft of intellectual property from U.S. targets since the announcement in September 2015 and how is the State Department, in conjunction with the rest of the U.S. Government, addressing these challenges?

Mr. BLINKEN. Thank you very much.

I think there are two things going on here. It's not a surprise that countries try to get information about other countries and that goes on every day and it continues to go on, of course, from China in the direction of the United States.

Where we've drawn a very bright line is on the question of using cyber technology to steal trade secrets for commercial advantage and a critical component of the agreement reached between President Obama and President Xi actually last fall and then reaffirmed is that China will no longer do that.

Now, it said that. It made a commitment. It's reasserted that, reaffirmed that in the G-20 as well as directly with us. We now have to make sure that that in fact is the case and it is being implemented.

So we are watching very vigilantly to see. I am not——

Mr. CICILLINE. But that is not my question. Has there—are you——

Mr. BLINKEN. I am not personally aware of cases—of current cases of that but I am happy to go back and confer with Admiral Rogers.

Mr. CICILLINE. Great. Thank you.

Next I'd like to turn to the issue of North Korea. In the wake of North Korea's recent nuclear weapons test and satellite launch, South Korean society has begun to reengage in the debate about developing its own nuclear weapons capability, even though, of course, Seoul relies on the U.S. nuclear umbrella. And I'd like to know whether you think there's support within the Korean Government for developing a nuclear capability and over the long term what should the United States' response be to this development?

Mr. BLINKEN. You're right that that debate has reemerged in South Korea as a result of North Korea's provocations. President Park was very clear in statements that she's made that that is not the path that South Korea should or will take, at least under her administration.

And we've tried to make clear to our allies and partners that it is not necessary because, to put it colloquially, we have their back with the nuclear umbrella and with every other means that we have to their defense.

So we have not only reaffirmed that very solemn commitment to the defense of Korea, we have strengthened our own relationship and one of the things that we've done is now engaged in formal consultations with them on deploying the THAAD missile defense system to South Korea and they're developing their own missile defense system in cooperation with us. So we've been building up the defenses including for our partners and allies and, of course, we've also been going very hard at the North Koreans on the nuclear missile program.

Mr. CICILLINE. Thank you.

And finally, Mr. Blinken, I'd like to turn to Malaysia. As you know well, there was significant concern about the upgrade of Malaysia to the Tier II watch list and I wondered if you could just speak a little bit to what progress Malaysia has made, particularly in the area of combating human trafficking, but in human rights as well as human trafficking since that time and whether or not we should—I mean, what progress has been made? I think you're aware of the controversy that is surrounding that change in their classification.

Mr. BLINKEN. As you know, Congressman, we are actually working very actively right now on the new report for this—for the past year and so I can't speak to its conclusions because they haven't been reached.

I can say generally with regard to Malaysia just over the past year some of the things we've seen. We have seen very significant and in fact unprecedented consultations between the government and civil society and international experts to draft regulations to implement the legal amendments that were passed by their Parliament at the very end of the last reporting period.

And that would really empower the agencies to enforce the amendments that were reached. So that is positive. That doesn't mean its dispositive of anything we'll conclude but it is something we've seen over the last year.

This would allow victims of trafficking to live and work outside shelters, which is a strong consideration. I know that we have remaining concerns about the conviction rate in Malaysia. That's something that we are looking at and that will factor in to the assessment and we need to continue to work with them to build their own capacity to investigate, to prosecute, to convict and we are doing that, for example, through IOM.

We are funding some of those activities. So I would say I can't speak to you, obviously, about the conclusions of the report. We haven't reached them yet. I would say based on this we've seen some progress but that is not dispositive to the conclusion.

Mr. CICILLINE. Well, can I just ask with respect to the implementation of one of the biggest issues then, virtually no prosecutions.

Mr. BLINKEN. Yes.

Mr. CICILLINE. So have you seen any progress on that? Enacting—it is one thing to enact and begin to implement but if it is not enforced it is sort of meaningless. Have you seen any progress on actual prosecutions?

Mr. BLINKEN. I agree with you. I agree with you on that. I mean, enforcement is a critical piece of this. I am not aware of significant progress on the prosecutions but I can come back to you on that.

Mr. CICILLINE. Great. I appreciate it so much.

Thank you, and I yield back, Mr. Chairman.

Chairman ROYCE. Mr. Matt Salmon of Arizona.

Mr. SALMON. Thank you.

Mr. Blinken, first, let me just go on record as saying how I commend the administration for pursuing deployment of THAAD in South Korea. I think it is incredibly important.

One of my frustrations is that many of these sanctions that we've done haven't really moved the needle with North Korea and I am not sure any other sanctions really will. I think that the one thing that will move North Korea is some flexing of the economic muscles by China and we've got to figure out a way to get them motivated because they haven't been—they helped us a little bit at the U.N., and I appreciate that with the multilateral sanctions. But they hold a disproportionate influence with North Korea than any of the rest of us or any of the other in the Six Party talks and we've got to influence them to do the right thing and get North Korea under control.

Last weekend, China announced that it formed a consensus with Brunei, Cambodia, and Laos that the territorial disputes over some islands, rocks, and shoals in the South China Sea are not an issue between China and the Association of Southeast Asian Nations—ASEAN—as a whole.

At the same time, China consistently relies on ASEAN's declaration on the conduct of parties in the South China Sea, citing its endorsement of consultations and negotiations to argue that it is not subject to the binding arbitration brought under the Law of the Sea Treaty by the Philippines.

Can China have it both ways? Is China trying to sideline ASEAN in relation to the South China Sea maritime disputes and what's the administration's response to the quadrilateral consensus between China, Brunei, Cambodia, and Laos and what's the administration's position on ASEAN's role in resolving the maritime disputes?

Mr. BLINKEN. Thank you very much.

And first of all, I very much appreciate your comments on North Korea and agree very much with you that China has a unique role to play because of its unique relationship with North Korea.

We are seeing some positive steps forward in terms of implementation of the Security Council resolution but it is not yet dispositive. So we are looking very carefully at that.

I could not agree more with you as well that China can't have it both ways. It can't have it both ways in a number of areas. It can't be a party to the Law of the Sea Convention and then ignore or reject the provisions of that treaty including arbitration as an appropriate mechanism and the binding nature of any arbitration decision on the parties to that decision.

So we would expect that China, as a party to the Law of the Sea Convention, once the decision is issued by the tribunal, will respect it. So it can't have it both ways there. It can't assert the Law of the Sea and not respect its decisions.

Second, with regard to ASEAN, I think you're exactly right. We worked very, very hard to build up ASEAN as an organization to make sure that it created a space in which countries that individually might not have the confidence to take on difficult issues like the South China Sea might feel some greater strength in numbers and collectively.

The President, as you know, had this historic summit with the ASEAN countries at Sunnylands just a few months ago. We are looking to ASEAN, as it did most recently at that summit, to express its support for these basic principles and we'd like to see that happen when the arbitration decision is issued as well.

And by the way, on the agreement that you referenced with Brunei and Laos, I think there is a lot less there than meets the eye.

Mr. SALMON. I hope so, and I hope that ASEAN really does step up to the plate when it comes to dealing with these maritime disputes and resolving them. I think the more they speak with one solid voice the better chance we have of resolving this without the conflicts that we hope we don't have.

My last point is that I am very optimistic about our economic opportunities in the region and I am a strong supporter of TPP. But I would also like to see us further enhance our trade ties with India and as such I have introduced legislation in concert with Senator Cornyn pushing for India's entrance into APEC.

What do you see as the obstacles to that getting done?

Mr. BLINKEN. First, we welcome India's interest in joining APEC and we also welcome, and I've said this directly to my Indian counterparts, talking to them about how they see membership in APEC fitting into their own thinking about their economy, about trade, and the evolution that they would make.

So I suspect we will have those conversations going forward. I also very much agree with the larger proposition that you cite about the importance of India and in particular the importance of trying to deepen and expand our own trade relationship with India and its own relations in the area.

I think a few things just in terms of obstacles. First of all, the other members, of course, would have to agree. It's a consensus-based organization. The other thing I'll tell you and I think, you know, this is a consideration as well. We want to make sure that as countries join organizations like APEC that they are going to work to productively and cooperatively to uphold its rules and standards and to be productive partners in that enterprise. So that is one of the things we'll be talking to the Indians about. But the bottom line is we welcome their interest and will be talking to them about it.

Mr. SALMON. Thank you.

Chairman ROYCE. Mr. Daniel Donovan from New York.

Mr. DONOVAN. Thank you, Mr. Chairman, and Secretary, thank you for your attendance and your testimony today.

In February of this year, the U.N. came out with a report about Vietnam making prohibited purchases of weapons from North Korea. As the President and this administration is about to enter into a trade agreement should their avoiding and actually unlawfully purchasing weapons from North Korea be a consideration as we enter into an agreement with Vietnam?

Mr. BLINKEN. We would be concerned with any country violating its obligations under the U.N. Security Council resolutions in terms of purchasing or making available to North Korea weapons, and if that is the case with Vietnam that is going to be a concern.

We are being very vigilant about making sure the countries are not doing that.

Mr. DONOVAN. And you also indicated about supplying North Korea with weapons. That same U.N. Council has indicated to us that Cuba is providing North Korea with illegal weapons. As the administration tries to renew relations with Cuba, should that be a consideration as we go forward?

Mr. BLINKEN. Yes. As you know, there was an incident in which a ship that was transporting weapons that apparently originated in Cuba and seemed to be heading for North Korea was actually stopped by the Panamanians and weapons were found on board. The weapons were confiscated. The ship was finally returned to the

North Korean ownership. There was, I think, a $700,000 fine that was paid. I think the captain was detained.

We've come down very hard at the United Nations on this shipment, including putting a spotlight on it—putting a spotlight on Cuba's apparent role in helping to facilitate this trade in weapons. This is a real concern and we've been very vigilant about making clear that that is unacceptable.

Mr. DONOVAN. And finally, Mr. Secretary, yesterday I met with steelworkers from my district. They're very concerned about China manipulating the steel market in the world.

We've had, I think, zero growth in steel production in our country over the last 25 years. I think Europe's steel production is down about 12 percent and there's a fear that China is manipulating by selling steel below market price in order to box everyone else out.

Is the State Department looking into that and what is the position of the administration?

Mr. BLINKEN. Congressman, I can say generally two things. First, my colleagues in the Treasury, Commerce, and USTR are across the board very vigilant about trade enforcement generally and with regard to China specifically.

We have, I think as you know, overall filed, I think, 20 WTO enforcement complaints since 2009—the most of any country. And by the way, we've won all of the cases that have been decided.

With regard to China specifically, and this is not in steel but this is more generally, just this past month they signed an agreement ending export subsidies as a result of a challenge we made to those subsidies at the WTO.

A year ago, we won a challenge to compliance on high-tech steel duties that we had challenged them on and that contributed to a $250 million annual loss to our exporters. That ended as a result of the enforcement actions that we took.

In 2014, there was a finding against China on duties and quotas on rare earths and tungsten. And finally, we issued—this again was the result of an action that we took. And also in 2014 there was a finding of breach regarding unjustified duties on cars and SUVs—$5.1 billion worth of cars and SUVs sold. There, too, we got a decision.

So I can't speak to the specific case that you referenced but I can promise you that I am sure my colleagues are looking at this very carefully and based on the record to date if there is something that is actionable we'll take action.

Mr. DONOVAN. Appreciate that, Mr. Secretary, because I know the American steelworkers would appreciate it as well if you and the administration could look into that.

Mr. Chairman, I yield back the rest of my time.

Chairman ROYCE. Thank you very much, Mr. Donovan.

We are at adjournment here. I do want to express our appreciation with the Deputy Secretary's time this morning and thanks for meeting with us after your recent trip back from Asia.

As we've discussed, the United States as a Pacific power has tremendous interests in Asia. We have allies in Asia. So we look forward to working with you on issues like the North Korean sanctions that I suggested. We need full implementation on that and on the transition in Burma, on the new government in Taiwan—

in Taipei. So many issues for us to continue to collaborate on and, Deputy Secretary, thank you again.

Mr. BLINKEN. Mr. Chairman, thank you very much.

Chairman ROYCE. We stand adjourned.

[Whereupon, at 11:57 a.m., the hearing was adjourned.]

APPENDIX

FULL COMMITTEE HEARING NOTICE
COMMITTEE ON FOREIGN AFFAIRS
U.S. HOUSE OF REPRESENTATIVES
WASHINGTON, DC 20515-6128

Edward R. Royce (R-CA), Chairman

April 28, 2016

TO: MEMBERS OF THE COMMITTEE ON FOREIGN AFFAIRS

You are respectfully requested to attend an OPEN hearing of the Committee on Foreign Affairs, to be held in Room 2172 of the Rayburn House Office Building (and available live on the Committee website at http://www.ForeignAffairs.house.gov):

DATE: Thursday, April 28, 2016

TIME: 10:00 a.m.

SUBJECT: America as a Pacific Power: Challenges and Opportunities in Asia

WITNESS: The Honorable Antony J. Blinken
Deputy Secretary of State
U.S. Department of State

By Direction of the Chairman

The Committee on Foreign Affairs seeks to make its facilities accessible to persons with disabilities. If you are in need of special accommodations, please call 202/225-5021 at least four business days in advance of the event, whenever practicable. Questions with regard to special accommodations in general (including availability of Committee materials in alternative formats and assistive listening devices) may be directed to the Committee.

COMMITTEE ON FOREIGN AFFAIRS
MINUTES OF FULL COMMITTEE HEARING

Day___*Thursday*___Date____*4/28/2016*____Room_____*2172*_____

Starting Time ____*10:08*____Ending Time ____*11:57*____

Recesses | *0* | (____to ____) (____to ____) (____to ____) (____to ____) (____to ____) (____to ____)

Presiding Member(s)

Chairman Edward R. Royce, Rep. Ileana Ros-Lehtinen

Check all of the following that apply:

Open Session ☑   Electronically Recorded (taped) ☑
Executive (closed) Session ☐   Stenographic Record ☑
Televised ☑

TITLE OF HEARING:

America as a Pacific Power: Challenges and Opportunities in Asia

COMMITTEE MEMBERS PRESENT:

See attached.

NON-COMMITTEE MEMBERS PRESENT:

HEARING WITNESSES: Same as meeting notice attached? Yes ☑ No ☐
(If "no", please list below and include title, agency, department, or organization.)

STATEMENTS FOR THE RECORD: *(List any statements submitted for the record.)*

IFR - Chairman Edward Royce
QFR - Ranking Member Eliot Engel
QFR - Rep. Ted Poe
QFR - Rep. Matt Salmon

TIME SCHEDULED TO RECONVENE _____
or
TIME ADJOURNED *11:57*_____

Jean Marter, Director of Committee Operations

HOUSE COMMITTEE ON FOREIGN AFFAIRS
FULL COMMITTEE HEARING

PRESENT	MEMBER	PRESENT	MEMBER
X	Edward R. Royce, CA	X	Eliot L. Engel, NY
X	Christopher H. Smith, NJ	X	Brad Sherman, CA
X	Ileana Ros-Lehtinen, FL	X	Gregory W. Meeks, NY
X	Dana Rohrabacher, CA	X	Albio Sires, NJ
X	Steve Chabot, OH	X	Gerald E. Connolly, VA
	Joe Wilson, SC	X	Theodore E. Deutch, FL
	Michael T. McCaul, TX		Brian Higgins, NY
X	Ted Poe, TX		Karen Bass, CA
X	Matt Salmon, AZ		William Keating, MA
	Darrell Issa, CA	X	David Cicilline, RI
	Tom Marino, PA		Alan Grayson, FL
	Jeff Duncan, SC	X	Ami Bera, CA
	Mo Brooks, AL	X	Alan S. Lowenthal, CA
	Paul Cook, CA		Grace Meng, NY
	Randy Weber, TX	X	Lois Frankel, FL
	Scott Perry, PA		Tulsi Gabbard, HI
	Ron DeSantis, FL		Joaquin Castro, TX
	Mark Meadows, NC		Robin Kelly, IL
X	Ted Yoho, FL		Brendan Boyle, PA
X	Curt Clawson, FL		
X	Scott DesJarlais, TN		
X	Reid Ribble, WI		
	Dave Trott, MI		
X	Lee Zeldin, NY		
X	Dan Donovan, NY		

174. The Panel has also confirmed that another designated individual, Kim Kwang Chun, played a key role in the shipment in 2012 of ballistic missile-related items seized by the Republic of Korea, while serving as the representative of Korea Tangun Trading Corporation in the Syrian Arab Republic (see annex 101 and S/2013/337, paras. 44-46, and S/2014/147, paras. 51-54). Two Member States reported that Mr. Kim was serving as representative of Ryungseng Trading Corporation (an alias of Tangun), based in Shenyang, China (see S/2015/131, para. 187).

F. Travel of individuals reportedly linked to designated entities

175. In 2015, the Panel investigated the travel activities of individuals designated by Member States or otherwise subject to Panel investigation as possibly working on behalf of designated entities.[89]

176. The Panel has obtained passport and air travel information on seven individuals designated by the United States as KOMID representatives or officials[90] (see table 8).

Table 8
Travel of reported KOMID representatives

Name	Date of birth	Passport number	Country in which reported as active
Mr. Jang Yong Son	20 February 1957	563110024	Islamic Republic of Iran
Mr. Kim Yong Chol	18 February 1962	472310168	Islamic Republic of Iran
Mr. Kang Ryong	18 February 1962	472310168	Syrian Arab Republic
Mr. Ryu Jin	21 August 1968	472410192	Syrian Arab Republic
Mr. Kil Jong Hun	7 August 1965	563410081	Namibia
Mr. Kim Kwang Yon	20 February 1972	472410022	Namibia
Mr. Jang Song Chol	30 July 1966	563210059	Russian Federation[a]

[a] The Russian Federation told the Panel that it opposed answering any inquiries based on unilateral sanctions (see annex 106).

177. The Panel has to date been unable to confirm that the above-listed individuals are KOMID representatives or officials. They transited through, entered or exited the following States between 2012 and September 2015: China, Egypt, Iran (Islamic Republic of), Malaysia, Singapore, Sudan, Uganda, United Arab Emirates and Zimbabwe (see annex 102). Those in the Islamic Republic of Iran and Namibia were confirmed as accredited diplomats by the United Arab Emirates, Pakistan and Namibia. Tourist or transit visas were provided to them for travel to the United Arab Emirates. Pakistan noted that their visa applications reflected an intention to visit

---

[89] See annex 102 for additional information on the global airlines project.
[90] United States Department of the Treasury, "Treasury imposes sanctions against the Government of the Democratic People's Republic of Korea", press release, 2 January 2015, available from www.treasury.gov/press-center/press-releases/Pages/jl9733.aspx.

Questions for the Record Submitted
To Deputy Secretary of State Antony J. Blinken
By Representative Ted Poe
House Foreign Affairs Committee
April 28, 2016

Question:
Earlier this week Congressman Rogers and I sent a letter to the Secretary of State, Secretary of Defense, and the Director of National Intelligence about likely Chinese support for Pakistan's ballistic missile program. Pakistan recently revealed its new medium-range nuclear ballistic missile carried on a 16-wheel transporter erector launcher, or "TEL". A leading specialist has noted the similarities between Pakistan's TEL and a TEL constructed by the China Aerospace Science and Industry Corporation (CASIC).

China has also provided a TEL to North Korea. Have State officials brought up this issue with the Chinese? Would such a transfer from China to Pakistan be subject to penalties as laid out in Sec. 72 and Sec. 73 of the Arms Export Control Act? What is the U.S. doing to counter China's proliferation of sensitive technologies to some of the worst actors in the world like Pakistan?

Answer:
In our bilateral discussions, we regularly engage with China on improving its export controls and on specific missile proliferation issues, including transfers of missile-related technology to programs of concern. While China has made progress over the years in the development of its export control system, missile programs of proliferation concern continue to obtain items from Chinese entities, and we continue to press China to stop such exports. In addition, we use our various domestic sanctions authorities as appropriate to address the proliferation activities of Chinese entities. We would be happy to discuss these issues in greater detail in a classified setting.

Question:
On March 17, senior State Department officials testified before the House Foreign Affairs Committee that U.S. officials were speaking to the French government to articulate that the French selling a large reprocessing plant to China would negatively impact the security interest of the U.S. and our allies.

Has State made this position clear to their Chinese counterparts? Do the French understand that making such a sale is not only at odds with our interests, but those of Japan and South Korea as well? Will the President raise this issue at the G7 meeting in Japan when he sees his French and Japanese counterparts?

Answer:
The United States has articulated its concerns to France about this potential sale to China, recognizing France's strong commitment to nonproliferation.

The United States has also made clear to China that we see China's recent announcement of its intent to work with French technology and investment to develop a commercial scale reprocessing plant as an important issue in the region. We will continue our existing dialogue with the Chinese government to learn more about its plans for the reprocessing plant.

We are not in a position to comment on what the President will raise this with his G-7 counterparts.

Question:
Several East Asian countries, such as China, Japan, and South Korea, have demonstrated interested in constructing plutonium reprocessing plants. If these countries were able to reprocess plutonium they would have to move it to other nuclear facilities spread throughout their respective countries. This could mean there would be trucks on the highway full of fissile material vulnerable to terrorist attacks or hijacking.

Do you support Secretary Moniz's recent statement in Beijing that China's decision to produce and stockpile plutonium for future civilian use is not a "positive" for nuclear nonproliferation and that the U.S. does not support commercial reprocessing? If so, what have you done to make this policy position clear to our partners in Asia?

Answer:
The United States has a longstanding policy of seeking to limit the further spread of sensitive fuel cycle technologies, including enrichment and reprocessing, to countries not already in possession of such technologies. Since reprocessing produces separated plutonium that, in principle, is able to be used to make nuclear weapons, our general view is that less reprocessing in the world is better than more.

We have an ongoing dialogue with our Asian partners regarding reprocessing and plutonium use and we will continue to do so.

Question:
The same plutonium reprocessing facilities from the previous question produce tons of plutonium that could potentially be used to make many nuclear weapons. Do you believe that it would be in our national security interest for Japan or South Korea to open these kinds of facilities?

Answer:
The United States has a long history of productive nuclear cooperation with Japan and the Republic of Korea (ROK) and a longstanding and ongoing dialogue across a wide range of nuclear nonproliferation, safety, and security issues, including reprocessing and plutonium use.

Our close cooperation on these issues gives us confidence that Japan and the ROK will continue to proceed in ways fully consistent with their nonproliferation obligations.

Question:
On April 25th, a Canadian man was beheaded in the southern Philippines by Abu Sayyaf gunmen, who have pledged allegiance to ISIS. Also that week, a rights activist in Bangladesh was hacked to death by a group affiliated with al Qaeda. Clearly Islamist terrorism has taken hold in Asia. What is the U.S. doing to combat the spread of such groups affiliated with ISIS and al Qaeda in the region?

Answer:
Governments across the region, including the Philippines and Bangladesh, actively seek to address threats and degrade the ability of terrorist groups to operate in their countries and in the region. In partnership with host governments, we work to strengthen counterterrorism legal frameworks, build partner capacity to investigate and prosecute terrorism cases, increase regional and bilateral

cooperation and information sharing, and address critical border and aviation security gaps.

As threats have changed – for example, the rising threat of foreign terrorist fighters – we've adapted our cooperation with regional governments, and we're always discussing new avenues. The Department's work on countering violent extremism (CVE) in particular seeks to reduce the ability of violent extremists to radicalize, recruit, and mobilize followers to violence and to address specific factors that feed violent extremist recruitment and radicalization. This includes working with USAID to build specific alternatives, programs, capabilities, and resiliencies in targeted communities and populations to reduce the risk of radicalization and recruitment.

Question:
Although most of the poachers are in Africa, Asia is where there is the highest demand for elephant ivory and rhino horn. If this demand isn't stopped, wildlife trafficking will only continue to get worse. What is the State Department doing to stem the demand for elephant ivory and rhino horn from Asia?

Answer:
The National Strategy for Combating Wildlife Trafficking has three strategic priorities, one of which is "Reduce Demand for Illegally Traded Wildlife." The National Strategy recognizes that increasing anti-poaching and anti-trafficking enforcement efforts will have only limited effect unless we work simultaneously to address the persistent demand that drives this trade. In addition to the Task Force and its member agencies efforts to reduce demand domestically, the Department of State, USAID, inter-agency partners, and civil society are working to promote demand reduction efforts globally.

Recognizing that some countries in Asia are a significant driver of demand for elephant ivory, rhino horn, and other trafficked wildlife and wildlife products, significant efforts and resources have been directed toward demand reduction in Asia.

In 2013 and 2015, the U.S. Fish and Wildlife Service crushed seized, contraband elephant ivory in two ivory crush events. The Department of State and
U.S. Embassies have promoted these events to audiences around the world, advocating for other countries to take similar actions. To date, 20 countries in total have joined us in destroying ivory, including China (and also the Hong Kong Special Administrative Region), Malaysia, the Philippines, Singapore, Sri Lanka, Thailand, and the United Arab Emirates. These events are sending a strong signal to ivory traffickers and their customers that we will not tolerate this illegal trade.

The U.S. government also actively pursued cooperation with governments and regional organizations to address wildlife trafficking. In one example from Asia, Chinese President Xi Jinping and President Obama in September 2015 agreed to enact nearly complete bans on ivory import and export, and to take significant and timely steps to halt the domestic commercial trade of ivory. To further raise public awareness, the Department of State published in Chinese (including Hong Kong) newspapers and websites Op-Eds commending these commitments and calling for their quick implementation, reaching tens of millions of Chinese citizens. We continue to engage China at multiple levels, including the U.S.-China Strategic and Economic Dialogue (S&ED). Our engagement with China also includes dialogue with Hong Kong, which recently announced its plans to implement an ivory ban.

Throughout Asia (and globally), U.S. Embassies are bringing together governments, NGOs, students, and celebrities in individual countries for visits and exchanges and to work to raise awareness and to stop the illegal trade in rhino horn and other wildlife products from protected species. In one recent example, the

U.S. Embassy in Vietnam, in partnership with the Government of Vietnam, the Government of South Africa, and civil society, launched Operation Game Change, a demand reduction campaign that included a series of public outreach events focused especially on reducing consumption of rhino horn. Launched on World Wildlife Day 2015, the campaign included the participation of Vietnamese Ministers and included multiple outreach events, such as awareness-raising bike rides led by the U.S. Ambassador and a film and concert festival called Wildfest that attracted approximately 2,500 people. The campaign effectively engaged key government officials, civil society, and business leaders, notably leading to a new partnership between Vietjet Airlines and the United States to reduce illegal wildlife consumption.

Efforts by USAID in 2015 to increase public awareness and concern also reached impressive numbers in countries like China, Vietnam, and Thailand. In China, for instance, USAID-supported public service announcements in transportation hubs, bus stations, and subways reached 23 million Chinese people daily. In Vietnam, a scorecard approach to monitoring the prevalence of wildlife crime at restaurants, pet shops, pharmacies and related businesses, as well as the success of authorities in addressing violations, resulted in a steady decline in wildlife crime in Hanoi and other cities since 2014. And in Thailand, 21 more hotels joined the Blue List of businesses pledging to refrain from serving shark fin, bringing the total to more than 180 businesses since the USAID-supported Fin Free Thailand campaign began in 2013.

For more information on the Task Force's efforts, refer to the 2015 Annual Progress Assessment available at http://www.state.gov/documents/organization/254013.pdf.

Question:

There is a long history of Iran and North Korea collaborating on their ballistic missile and nuclear programs. With North Korea getting more and more belligerent with their missile and nuclear tests, what is the U.S. doing to prevent the development of this perilous relationship between two bad actors?

Answer:

The United States continues to work closely with our partners and the international community to address the threats posed by North Korea's nuclear and ballistic missile programs. The United States closely monitors and reviews all available information on North Korea's weapons of mass destruction programs and its proliferation activities worldwide, including any efforts to provide Iran with proliferation-sensitive materials or technologies.

We continue to take concerted steps, both unilateral and multilateral, to impede North Korea's proliferation activities, including through the imposition and enforcement of sanctions under relevant U.S. authorities, and United Nations Security Council resolutions concerning North Korea.

We also continue to closely monitor Iran's activities to ensure they are consistent with Iran's nuclear commitments under the Joint Comprehensive Plans of Action (JCPOA) and with the requirements of UN Security Council resolution 2231 (2015). We have been clear with Iran that the sanctions relief provided under the JCPOA is contingent on Iran's continued fulfillment of its nuclear-related commitments for their full duration.

Question:

In April 2013, the Director of the DIA testified that that Syria's missile program depends on essential foreign equipment and assistance, primarily from North Korean entities. Additionally, in July 2014, press reports indicated that Hamas attempted to negotiate a new arms deal with North Korea for missiles and communications equipment. On December 19, 2014, the Federal Bureau of Investigation concluded that North Korea was responsible for the cyber-attack on Sony Pictures Entertainment.

For these reasons and many others, why is North Korea not back on the State Sponsors of Terrorism list?

Answer:
As a matter of law, in order for any country to be designated as a State Sponsor of Terrorism (SST), the Secretary of State must determine that the government of that country has *repeatedly* provided support for acts of international terrorism. These designations are made after careful review of all available evidence to determine if a country meets the statutory criteria for designation.

We regularly review all of the available intelligence on the Democratic People's Republic of Korea (DPRK) to determine whether it meets the statutory criteria for designation as a State Sponsor of Terrorism.

Even without being designated an SST, North Korea remains among the most heavily sanctioned countries in the world. We continue to take concerted efforts, both nationally and multilaterally, to impede the DPRK's proliferation activities, including through the use of the full suite of relevant
U.S. unilateral sanctions measures and by urging all countries to implement relevant United Nations Security Council resolutions concerning the DPRK.

Moreover, the United States continues to work closely with the international community and our partners to address the global security and proliferation threat posed by the DPRK's nuclear and ballistic missile programs. The United States closely monitors and reviews all available information on the DPRK's dealings related to its weapons of mass destruction programs and its proliferation activities worldwide.

Regarding the Sony cyber hack, the President characterized the event as a very serious act of cyber vandalism to which the United States responded proportionately.

The White House has stated that one piece of that response was Executive Order 13687, signed by the President on January 2, 2015 – a broad, powerful new sanctions authority that gives the United States much greater flexibility to target the DPRK regime, ruling party, and their supporters.

Question:
China recently unveiled a plan to build floating nuclear plants in the South China Sea to provide power to the artificial islands they are illegally building there. What does this mean for China's power projection in the area, and what should the U.S. do to address this plan? Has diplomacy with China been at all effective in combatting China's aggressive stance in the South China Sea?

Answer:
We are aware of reports suggesting China is exploring the development of floating nuclear reactors for use in the South China Sea. However, these reports are unconfirmed, and the timeline for developing and deploying this technology is unclear. We will continue monitoring Chinese efforts to upgrade and expand their outposts in the Spratly Islands, including the potential for future deployments of this technology.

We continue to encourage all claimants to avoid taking unilateral actions that change the status quo, to clarify their maritime claims in accordance with international law, as reflected in the Law of the Sea Convention, and to commit to peacefully manage or resolve their disputes.

Question:

Has there been any new information on North Korea's most recent nuclear test? Has it been determined that it was boosted fission and not a hydrogen detonation?

Answer:

North Korea's UN-proscribed nuclear weapons and missile programs continue to pose a serious threat to the United States, our allies, and the security environment in East Asia. On January 6, 2016, North Korea conducted a nuclear test, which it claimed was the successful test of a "hydrogen bomb." The low yield of the test is not consistent with a successful test of a thermonuclear device.

We can provide additional information on this issue in a classified setting.

Question:

What does North Korea's recent submarine-launched ballistic missile test mean for the security of U.S. allies in the region? Although the test was a failure, what more can the U.S. do to counter this dangerous posturing given that sanctions will not be wholly effective unless China fully commits to enacting them?

Answer:

North Korea's UN-proscribed nuclear weapons and missile programs continue to pose a serious threat to the United States, our allies, and the security environment in East Asia.

On April 23, North Korea launched a submarine-launched ballistic missile (SLBM), which failed. Regardless, this launch constitutes a clear and significant violation of multiple UN Security Council resolutions. All launches contribute to the technical advancement of North Korea's UN-proscribed ballistic missile program. Further information can be provided in a closed setting.

The United States and China agree on the fundamental importance of a denuclearized North Korea, and we welcomed China's agreement on UN Security Council resolution 2270, which includes the strongest sanctions the Security Council has imposed in a generation.

We will continue to urge China to do more to exert its unique leverage until we see concrete signs that Kim Jong Un has come to the realization that the only viable path forward for his country is denuclearization.

Questions for the Record Submitted
To Deputy Secretary of State Antony Blinken
By Representative Eliot L. Engel
House Foreign Affairs Committee
April 28, 2016

Question:

Given U.S. national interest in Asia, is the EAP Bureau being given sufficient priority to carry out its mission? With the current challenges in the budget environment, has the Department been willing to make hard choices to reallocate funding from other priorities to resource the "Rebalance?"

Answer:

Other regions may have contingencies causing their budgets to fluctuate from year to year, but with the help of Congress, EAP has seen steady growth since the beginning of the Obama Administration. However, for several budget cycles,
EAP's actual discretionary funding has been cut relative to the President's request. Additionally, while we have been able to meet the strategic needs of the
Rebalance, additional flexibility would assist in effective program implementation.

The FY 2017 President's Request provides $1.5 billion to support the Rebalance, which reflects a $100 million increase over FY 2015. This 6.7 percent increase is a clear signal of the importance of the Rebalance and our commitment to the region.

Question:

What steps has the Administration taken to translate the Rebalance into a cohesive across-the-government plan to ensure that Asia receives higher priority across the federal government? Has our normal policymaking system proven sufficient to facilitate a more strategic "whole of government" approach?

Answer:

The Administration engages in comprehensive strategic planning to ensure the Rebalance is implemented at all levels of government. U.S. government agencies in close coordination with our international partners are implementing an integrated, "forward-deployed" diplomacy and development strategy. In 2016, the Bureau of East Asian and Pacific Affairs (EAP) updated its Joint Regional Strategy (JRS), a high-level strategic document that lays out broad goals and lines of effort within the region. Through a number of interagency consultations on the Administration's overall Rebalance strategy, the Department of State, USAID and other U.S. government agencies jointly formulated a strategy to deepen U.S. strategic engagement and enhance America's leadership role to influence and benefit from a rising Asia-Pacific.

The Department, together with U.S. Embassies in Asia, coordinate interagency groups to develop country level "whole of government" strategies developed by embassy country teams. The Embassy strategies align the high level strategic goals of the JRS with results oriented programming and host government cooperation. The process ensures a careful government-wide Rebalance policy that is solidly grounded with in-country expertise.

Question:

Has the Administration's policy, including quarterly freedom of navigation operations in the South

China Sea, slowed China's expansion of their control over disputed landmasses and waters in the South China Sea? Has the policy enabled our partners and allies as they seek to push back against Chinese incursions into their territorial claims? How has U.S. strategy shifted, if at all, in response to steadily escalating tensions?

Answer:

The Administration employs a comprehensive and multifaceted approach to the South China Sea:

First, the United States consistently shines a spotlight on problematic behavior that raises tensions and complicates the situation in the South China Sea, particularly activities that threaten the freedom of navigation. The U.S. also raises this issue regularly in multilateral fora, such as the ASEAN Regional Forum and East Asia Summit, to emphasize the importance of peace and stability.

Second, we are strengthening maritime domain awareness and law enforcement capabilities in the region. This includes new security cooperation agreements with allies and partners in Southeast Asia and providing equipment and training to help partners better patrol their waters.

Third, we are engaging in intense, high-level diplomacy with China. President Obama, Secretary Kerry, and Defense Secretary Carter continue to make our interests and concerns clear to the Chinese in an open and frank manner.

Fourth, we are advocating for peaceful dispute resolution and international law. We have consistently called on all parties to negotiate a Code of Conduct in the South China Sea, which would build on the Declaration on the Conduct they made in 2002. The U.S. calls for all claimants to respect and adhere to international law, particularly the Law of the Sea, especially when it comes to making and pursuing territorial and maritime claims. We also express support for the right of any country to use international legal mechanisms, including arbitration, that are available to them, just as the Philippines has done.

Finally, the U.S. is strengthening our defensive presence in the South China Sea. As part of a long term strategy, we are moving 60 percent of our Naval fleet to the Pacific and rotating more of our forces through friendly countries in the region.

The United States has also, through our Freedom of Navigation operations and overflights, made very clear that we intend to ensure the South China Sea remains an open body of water where all countries all countries have the right to fly, sail, and operate wherever international law allows.

Our relationships throughout the region are strengthening, support for a common vision of a rules-based regional order is deepening, and demand for us to play a more active role in upholding regional stability is increasing.

If China sought to deflect international attention away from the South China Sea while it carried out its activities, then it has failed. In fact, the region and international community are increasingly vocal against activities that raise tensions and complicate the situation. In February, ASEAN leaders joined the President in calling for disputes to be resolved peacefully, with full respect for diplomatic and legal processes. The United States and ASEAN Member States also stressed the importance of international law, including the freedoms of navigation and overflight. These messages have been echoed elsewhere, most recently by the G-7.

There is growing demand for greater U.S. security presence in the region, as well greater interest in economic diversification and expanded security ties with other regional leaders. The real question with regard to the South China Sea is not about turning reefs into military bases, but whether the other claimants insist on a rules-based system that is fair to countries of all sizes.

Question:

Given China's rapid modernization and expansion of its Coast Guard and Naval capabilities, are current levels of security assistance to Southeast Asian partners sufficient? Do they significantly change the South China Sea strategic picture?

Answer:

The Department is committed to increasing the maritime security capacities of our partners in the region. Our security assistance to the region has been increasing in recent years, and Southeast Asian countries have recognized our strong commitment to helping them bolster their maritime capabilities. In November 2015, the White House released a Fact Sheet detailing the numerous U.S. efforts to build maritime capacity in Southeast Asia. In May, we hosted Coast Guard officials from Indonesia, Malaysia, the Philippines, and Vietnam at the Joint Interagency Task Force-South (JIATF-S) where they learned how JIATF-S develops international partnerships and works through the interagency process to execute its mission. We are also coordinating closely with our strong allies Japan and Australia to leverage our respective security assistance programs for Southeast Asian partners.

We continuously assess partners' equipment and training requirements and their institutional capacity to induct, employ, and maintain new equipment. Our assistance thus signals our commitment to upholding the rules-based order that continues to bring stability and prosperity in the region, and our partners, armed with the capabilities that our equipment and training provide, contribute to that rules-based order.

Question:

Did these authorities duplicate authorities and appropriations under State's FMF program, or do they complement existing programs? How does the United States coordinate its security assistance programs to promote a broader strategy to promote stability in the South China Sea?

Answer:

Section 1263 of the FY 2016 NDAA, known as the Maritime Security Initiative, provides DoD the authority to conduct security sector assistance activities that could be conducted under existing Department of State authorities, particularly foreign military financing (FMF). The Departments of State and Defense work together to ensure that our efforts are complementary.

Question:

In 2013, Chinese President Xi Jinping called for China to build an overland "Silk Road Economic Belt" and a sea-based "21st Century Maritime Silk Road." Together the initiatives are known as the "Belt and Road Initiatives." They represent an ambitious effort on China's part to boost development and economic connectivity among dozens of countries on at least three continents, and in so doing, to create "strategic propellers" for China's own economic development.

What impact do you see China's Belt and Road Initiatives having on the geopolitical landscape of Central, South, and Southeast Asia? In what ways do the initiatives challenge U.S. interests?

Answer:

China's One Belt, One Road (OBOR) encompasses a range of Chinese initiatives across South and Central Asia (and beyond) that aim to foster regional economic connectivity through new transport infrastructure, the construction of industrial corridors, investments in ports, and new trade routes. Currently, OBOR remains more of an organizing concept than an actual blueprint, and even Chinese officials are uncertain as to its exact geographic or strategic scope.

The United States supports positive relations among countries in Central, South, and Southeast Asia, and we are, in general, a strong proponent of economic and cultural connections.

Question:
What is the United States strategic approach to China's efforts to create an increasingly integrated East, Central, and South Asia? How do you see the Belt and Road Initiatives relating to U.S.-backed initiatives such as New Silk Road?

Answer:
China has said that one major objective of OBOR is to improve infrastructure across South and Central Asia. We recognize that there are enormous infrastructure needs in the region, and greater connectivity can potentially benefit everyone, including the United States. We have encouraged China to align its infrastructure projects and assistance with the needs of recipient countries, and with global standards for infrastructure investment. As details of China's initiative become clearer, we remain open to working with the Chinese government and with recipients in South and Central Asia and to exploring how China's investment in the region may be complementary to our cooperation with our partners in the New Silk Road initiative.

Question:
Since the September 2015 agreement, are you aware of cases in which the Chinese government may have supported cyber-enabled theft of intellectual property from U.S. targets? How is the State Department, in coordination with the rest of the U.S. government, addressing the challenge?

Answer:
We continue to monitor China's cyber activities closely and press China to abide by and fully implement the commitments reached during President Xi's state visit last September. We have been clear with the Chinese government that we are watching to ensure their words are matched by actions. We will continue to use all of the tools at our disposal to protect our networks and our citizens against cyber threats.

Question:
Given the National League of Democracy (NLD)'s landslide victory in the parliamentary elections, some argue that the U.S. government should eliminate or waive some or all of the remaining restrictions on relations with Burma. Others point to the Burmese military's substantial power in the new government (25% of the seats in parliament, virtual autonomy from civilian oversight, and control over all the nation's security forces) as evidence that Burma's transition to a democracy is incomplete and, therefore, it is premature to further remove restrictions on relations.

What do you see as a prudent U.S. policy on restrictions on relations with Burma? Is it time to review or rationalize our sanctions policy with respect to Burma, and if so, what changes would you propose?

Answer:
During decades of rule by the Burmese military, the U.S. government established a

comprehensive set of economic sanctions and other restrictions. The goal was to change behavior: encourage democratic reform, encourage respect for human rights, and incentivize sustainable economic development.

Following the initial implementation of democratic reforms and improved human rights protections in 2012, the U.S. government began a calibrated easing of sanctions. In November 2015, Burma held its first democratic elections in 50 years, and in April 2016, established a civilian government led through a peaceful transfer of power. At the same time, significant democracy and human rights challenges remain, including, as you note, the continuing disproportionate role of the military in the government and the economy, ongoing conflict with certain ethnic armed groups, and significant discrimination against certain ethnic and religious minorities, including the Rohingya.

Going forward, we will continue to look for ways to encourage further reform and demonstrate our support for the new government using all diplomatic tools available. Measures could include further calibration of our sanctions regime, the adoption of policies that will encourage the expansion of bilateral trade and investment, adding Burma as a beneficiary country under the Generalized System of Preferences (GSP), and expanded technical assistance consistent with applicable law.

We look forward to continued consultations with Congress and others stakeholders as we consider how best support political and economic reform in Burma.

Question:

National Security Advisor Susan Rice recently announced a proposed expansion of the President's Malaria Initiative in an effort to eliminate malaria from Cambodia entirely. How will Malaria elimination in Cambodia help address artemisinin resistance in the broader Mekong Delta sub-region?

Answer:

Eliminating malaria in Cambodia will help address artemisinin resistance in the Greater Mekong Subregion (GMS). In February, National Security Advisor Rice announced the Administration's plans for programming a $200 million increase requested for malaria as part of the Administration's FY 2017 budget request. These plans include expanding malaria efforts in Cambodia to accelerate progress toward malaria elimination, aligned with the Cambodia National Malaria Control program's stated goal of achieving malaria elimination by 2025. The Administration's proposal responds to a call by the global malaria community to eliminate malaria in GMS to directly address the threat of artemisinin

resistance. The President's Malaria Initiative (PMI) believes that prioritizing the push toward elimination in Cambodia will produce experience to be applied to elimination efforts across the GMS, with the goal of elimination of malaria in all countries in the region no later than 2030. Ultimately eliminating artemisinin resistance from the region will remove the threat that presently exists of resistance spreading from the GMS countries to other parts of the world.

Artemisinin-based combination therapies are the first-line treatment for malaria in almost all malaria-affected countries worldwide. Resistance to artemisinin was first identified in Cambodia in an area bordering Thailand almost a decade ago, and has since been identified in other countries of the GMS, including Burma, Cambodia, China (Yunnan Province), Lao PDR, Thailand, and Vietnam. The identification of resistance in countries of the GMS has raised fears among the global malaria community that artemisinin resistance could spread beyond the GMS into higher burden malaria areas, particularly sub-Saharan Africa. In the 1960s and 1970s, resistance to chloroquine, the first-line malaria treatment at the time, arose also in the Thai-Cambodian border region and subsequently spread globally. Chloroquine resistance is considered one of the key factors that led to the failure of malaria eradication efforts during that era and also resulted in a significant resurgence of malaria cases and deaths in sub-Saharan Africa during the latter part of the 20th century. Therefore, addressing artemisinin drug resistance in the GMS is imperative and the only solution to prevent the spread of artemisinin resistance to other parts of the world.

This call for elimination is bolstered by the significant progress that has been made in GMS countries to reduce malaria transmission by effective malaria programming, including distribution of insecticide-treated bed nets and rapid diagnosis and treatment of malaria cases. Cambodia, for example, through support from PMI and other partners, has experienced significant progress in reducing malaria. Malaria cases have steadily reduced to only approximately 35,000 cases reported in 2015, with only 10 recorded deaths. One district prioritized by PMI for elimination, Sampov Loun, in the border region with Thailand, has reported a steady reduction in cases over time, with only 250 cases reported last year, of which only 50 were acquired locally. This translates into less than two percent of the district population now infected with malaria. Such evidence provides support that Cambodia's goal of eliminating malaria by 2025 is achievable, if sufficient resources and effort are focused on elimination program implementation. With additional U.S. Government resources, PMI will expand the number of districts where intensified malaria elimination efforts can be supported, resulting in an acceleration of progress toward achieving overall elimination in Cambodia. PMI's efforts in Thailand and Burma also continue to focus on driving down malaria transmission toward elimination, and lessons from the prioritized elimination push in Cambodia will be applied to efforts in Thailand, Burma and more broadly in the Mekong region.

Question:
Has the State Department, who similarly has personnel serving in high-risk/high- threat, non-permissive and conflict environments, undertaken a similar review? If so, what were the results of this study? If not, why not?

Answer:
The Department of State's Office of Medical Services (MED) includes a robust Mental Health Services (MHS) program that is integrated with the core medical program. MED/MHS includes a leadership and support group based in Washington, D.C., as well as 20 Regional Psychiatrists (RMOPs) posted at embassies around the world. These psychiatrists provide direct patient care and consultation to the employees and family members throughout their respective regions as well as develop local sources of care. The program is constantly evolving and monitored through a variety of internal and external review processes making this type of top to bottom review unnecessary.

Question:
Since 2002, what countries have been designated as non-permissive, high- risk/high-threat, or critical priority countries – or received some other comparable designation to denote that they are high operational stress environments for State, USAID and other non-DoD civilian workers, including contractors? Please specify which country or part of the country received which designations and for what period of time. Include information for U.S. individuals operating under the authority of the Chief of Mission (as opposed to a Geographic Combatant Commander).

Answer:
In 2013, the Department created the High Threat Programs Directorate within the Bureau of Diplomatic Security and designated diplomatic posts housed within that Directorate as High Threat,

High Risk (HTHR). The list of these posts is sensitive and therefore cannot be discussed in this setting. We are willing to provide you with additional information in a briefing.

"Critical priority countries" (CPC) is a USAID designation. Since 2004, these countries are identified by USAID on an annual basis as being the highest priority to fill. For the last several years, these countries have remained the same: Afghanistan, Iraq, Pakistan, and South Sudan. Assignments to these posts are for one year, are unaccompanied, and staff receive hardship and danger differentials/allowances. In the past, Yemen and Libya were also listed. However, since there is no permanent Embassy presence in these two counties at this time, they have been removed from the list.

USAID defines an Non-permissive Environment (NPE) country as having significant barriers to USAID operating effectively and safely due to one or more of the following factors: armed conflict to which the U.S. is a party or not a party; limited physical access due to distance, disaster, geography, or non-presence; restricted political space due to repression of political activity and expression; or uncontrolled criminality including corruption.

Due to the sensitivity, the countries currently designated by USAID as NPE cannot be listed in this setting.

Question:

Who makes these determinations? Please explain the Department's process and enumerate the factors considered. How frequently are the designations reviewed?

Answer:

In March 2013, the Department developed a list of high threat, high risk (HTHR) posts, considering a variety of factors. The Department refreshes this list at a minimum annually and uses it as a tool to assist in ensuring HTHR posts receive necessary support. The High Threat Post Review Board is comprised of the Bureaus of Diplomatic Security and Intelligence and Research, regional bureaus, the Executive Secretariat, the Operations Center Crisis Management Support, Office of Management Policy Right-sizing and Initiative (M/PRI), and representatives from the Under Secretary for Management, Deputy Secretary and Deputy Secretary for Management and Resources. The Secretary of State ultimately approves this list each year.

Critical Priority Countries (CPCs) and Non-permissive Environments (NPEs) are USAID designations related to personnel assignments and USAID operations within a country, respectively. CPC and NPE are internal designations made by USAID and do not necessarily refer to the security situation at a Post.

The Department is available to provide a briefing on the aforementioned designations.

Question:

How many State Foreign Service officers and civil service employees are currently or have previously served in high-threat, non-permissive, critical priority countries, or conflict environments? Of these, how many have served for a cumulative period of 3 years or more, either as an assignment or temporary duty assignment.
Please provide this data by:

   a.) Agency (State, USAID, USDA, etc.)

   b.) Type of Personnel (hiring authority or category such as Foreign Service Officer, Civil Servant, Personal Services Contractor , etc.)

c.) TDY or assignment

Answer:

Department of State Foreign Service employees sign up to serve worldwide and be available to meet the needs of the Department. This often requires employees to serve in an unaccompanied post or face hardships overseas. For the Foreign Service, employees need to serve in differential posts as a requirement for advancement into the Senior Foreign Service. One way to meet this requirement is to serve in a Priority Service Post (PSP). PSP have included the following countries: Afghanistan, Iraq, Pakistan, Libya or Yemen.   Overall, 15 percent of present career full-time permanent Department of State employees (combined Civil Service and Foreign Service) have a record of service in a PSP. This figure includes 21 percent of Foreign Service Officers, 30 percent of Foreign Service Specialists, and one percent of civil service who have served in a PSP. We also have contractors at those posts that are under the authority of their hiring bureau.

The current tour of duty to these countries is typically one year, so there are a few employees with 3 or more years of service.

The Department can provide a briefing to discuss the different differentials and service needs of the Department.

Question:

What mental health or resilience support is provided in-country, including for ongoing stress resulting from the operating and for acute traumatic events?

Answer:

The Office of Medical Services/Mental Health Services (MED/MHS) has a multi-leveled approach to support for employees and families posted in high threat, high conflict posts beginning at the point of contact in the field and reaching back to additional resources domestically.

First, MED's Deployment Stress Management Program (DSMP) engages employees and family members before, during, and after deployment to high stress posts. These clinicians have partnered with the Foreign Service Institute (FSI) to provide routine briefings prior to deployment to inoculate and educate employees regarding what to expect and provide guidance on resiliency techniques. Once deployed, the employees and family members have access to MED/MHS regional psychiatrists assigned throughout the world; every embassy health unit knows how to contact their respective Regional Medical Officer/Psychiatrist (RMOP). Indeed, RMOPs routinely visit all posts in their region on a regular basis, regardless of whether there is a crisis or not. All RMOPs have video conference capability in their offices, allowing immediate engagement with patients who may be geographically distant. These Digital Video Conferencing (DVC) units are stand- alone terminals that communicate encrypted information through the closed Department of State intranet system. Finally, MED/MHS also has assigned Social Workers to Kabul, Baghdad, and Islamabad. These social workers coordinate consultative care with the RMOPs posted in their respective regions.

Question:

What assessments or screenings are conducted for employees or contractors returning from countries with the distinctions high-threat, non-permissive, critical priority countries, or conflict environments? Are these assessments or screenings mandatory or voluntary?

Answer:

Currently all employees departing from the following countries: Pakistan, Iraq, Afghanistan, South Sudan, and Central African Republic are required to take the Foreign Service Institute (FSI) course "High Threat Assignment Outbriefing Program" which addresses post-tour issues including expected adjustment issues and resiliency updating. Those identified with adjustment or possible stress related disorders are then referred to the appropriate care setting to include in house therapists assigned to the Deployment Stress Management Program (DSMP). In addition, employees completing tours in Iraq, Afghanistan, and Pakistan are strongly encouraged to participate in an outbrief with a Mental Health Services (MHS) therapist prior to leaving post. Post-deployment, DSMP staff email all employees immediately after leaving post and 30, 90, and 180 days thereafter to keep the connection to care open and follow up on problems that may emerge post deployment.

Question:

What mental health or support services are available for civilians? Of these services, which, if any, are mandatory? Which are discretionary?

Answer:

All Department of State employees and family members posted abroad have access to mental health services as described above, under the auspices of their embassy or consulate health unit. Other than the mandatory screenings for those departing from Pakistan, Iraq, Afghanistan, South Sudan, and Central African Republic, none of these services are mandatory. Department of State mental health providers position themselves in as much of a patient advocate role as possible with the top priority being the provision optimal mental health care in a safe and confidential setting.

Question:

The 2015 QDDR stated that, "The Department and USAID will ensure that we continue to balance our values and interests with the inherent risks of 21st-century diplomacy and development. We will encourage a broad dialogue on physical risk with the Executive and Legislative branches and beyond, recognizing that we cannot stop all threats. In consultation with Congress, our interagency partners, and other stakeholders, we will seek ways to streamline operations and increase flexibility in dangerous environments, and we will implement the Department's risk-management policy. Additionally, we will continue to develop skilled, professional leaders and managers with the judgment to make tough calls and to trust their people to do the same."

What is the Department doing to reevaluate risk?

Answer:

The Quadrennial Diplomacy and Development Review (QDDR) is an ongoing and important dialog that must take into account the increasingly complex world in which we operate. This means addressing risks to personnel, facilities, and operations but also the risks of disengagement. We are constantly assessing and evaluating risk and how to balance with the demands of our business, and appreciate Congressional interest and partnership on our efforts.

In March 2015, the Department published a formal Risk Management Policy (2 FAM 030) that emphasized advancing U.S. foreign policy objectives involves diverse types of risk and requires employees to engage in risk management for the decisions and activities within the scope of their duties. A central goal of the new risk management policy is to guide employees as they identify, manage, and mitigate risks in developing policy and implementing programs. Since the guidance was published, the Department has worked to institutionalize the new policy and implement a standard approach for managing and mitigating risk across our work overseas through the Vital Presence Validation Process (VP2). The Department has also launched an internal review to examine the challenges and issues we face in formulating policy and best practices executing operations in the highest risk environments. This review is working to update and reform the tools and processes that are needed to make our people, our platforms, our policies and processes as effective, flexible, collaborative, and agile.

We continually discuss these issues with Congress and other agencies with presence overseas. Secretary Kerry has raised the issue of the risks and dangers inherent in conducting diplomacy and development in his speeches as well as conversations with Congressional members. Deputy Secretary Higginbottom has also highlighted this issue in recent remarks to public audiences. In line with the QDDR recommendation, we are currently planning additional engagement with Congress, the private sector, NGOs partners and others about the realities of our work and the way we manage risk.

Question:

Leadership was listed as a key area of focus in the 2015 QDDR (pp.71, and 73-74), however, "leadership, management, and supervision" was also highlighted as a primary stressor in the 2015 USAID Assessment Report cited above.

Have the Department and/or USAID conducted any managerial climate surveys or taken other actions to address this issue? If not, what plans does the Department have to do so in the future?

Answer:

The Department adopted the Secretary's Leadership and Management Principles as a core foundation for leadership, professional development, and employee engagement. The Culture of Leadership initiative, a combined effort from multiple bureaus, promotes and operationalizes these principles, which are incorporated into employee performance assessments. We use the Federal Employee Viewpoint Survey and have instituted a centrally managed exit surveying system (that enables separating employees to comment on their experiences) and other engagement surveys to improve human resource management and strategic planning in the Department. These surveys target, inter alia, work-life balance and leadership.

The Bureau of Human Resources has put leadership, professional development, employee engagement, and diversity as priority objectives as it reviews, re-validates and reforms programs and policies to recruit, retain, and sustain a talented, diverse, and capable workforce equipped for the today's challenges and those of 2025 and beyond. The Foreign Service Institute's (FSI) Leadership & Management School (FSI/LMS) has begun work on a new Leadership Development Continuum, which when completed, will incorporate continuous and blended learning, online modules, and other

21st century industry- standard methods of adult instruction so that it is relevant to each employee; provides opportunities for continuous, ongoing improvement; taps and unleashes the talents of the Department's entire workforce; produces greater organizational effectiveness; and fosters a stronger, more resilient culture of leadership within the Department. FSI/LMS also recently launched the Entry Level Supervisor/Singleton (ELS) training, a pilot program designed to ensure first-tour, Foreign Service supervisors, generalists and specialists, have the skills required to effectively lead and manage a team at an overseas post. ELS is FSI's first blended and continuous learning program to incorporate classroom learning, coaching, mentoring, as well as both synchronous and asynchronous virtual learning. After the pilot phase concludes, we hope to scale up the program. Finally, FSI/LMS has realigned existing resources to expand access for the Civil and Foreign Service to its coaching program.

The design of the new Leadership Development Continuum will be informed by an independent, outside Leadership Training Needs Assessment, Audit and Benchmarking Study, which should be completed in early 2017. In addition, we use the Federal Employee Viewpoint Survey and have instituted a centrally managed exit surveying system (that enables separating employees to comment on their experiences) and other engagement surveys to improve human resource management and strategic planning in the Department. These surveys target, inter alia, work-life balance, leadership. All new Foreign Service and Civil Service supervisors, regardless of rank, are now required to take mandatory supervisory training within 12 months of becoming a supervisor. In June, FSI/LMS will launch the distance learning version of this supervisory training, Fundamentals of Supervision, which will make it easier for supervisors worldwide to access this training. Starting at the GS-13/FS-3 level, employees are required to take FSI's mandatory leadership classes at the appropriate level for their responsibilities and grade. Once Department employees cross over the senior executive threshold, they are required to take the Senior Executive Threshold Seminar. In addition, FSI offers job-specific leadership training to all new Deputy Chiefs of Mission and to all Ambassadors.

Question:

What training, including safety and resilience training, is currently provided for civilians deploying to high-threat, non-permissive, critical priority countries, or conflict environments? Is this training mandatory or discretionary? What proportion of personnel complete the training?

Answer:

The Department has instituted a range of mandatory and highly recommended courses to prepare our personnel to serve in the most challenging posts around the world. The Foreign Service Institute (FSI) and the Diplomatic Security (DS) Training Center provide a series of courses for foreign affairs professionals assigned to U.S. diplomatic posts overseas designated as High Threat High Risk (HTHR) posts. Given today's operating environment, these courses include training on safety and security, personal and community resilience, crisis preparation, and techniques for carrying out diplomacy in spite of the security restrictions and conflict environments. Below is a breakdown of the mandatory and highly recommended training for HTHR posts. Training courses below run pre-assignment, during assignment, and post assignment.

Mandatory Pre-assignment Training:

- All personnel assigned under Chief of Mission authority or present at one or combination of HTHR Posts for more than 45 days must complete the Foreign Affairs Counter Threat (FACT) course, offered by the DS Training Center. This is a five-day course. Each course includes an integrated module on personal resilience. The Department is in the process of making this a mandatory course for all posts overseas, regardless of location. FACT is also available for Eligible Family Members (EFMs) to take on a space- available basis. The High Threat Security Overseas Seminar is a mandatory online course for U.S. government executive branch personnel and employed EFMs serving under Chief of Mission authority in HTHR on a TDY assignment of less than 45 days.
- All personnel assigned to Afghanistan must complete Afghanistan Familiarization.

- All personnel assigned to Iraq must complete Iraq Familiarization.
- The Department's approved program designed to meet the requirements of all executive agencies that deploy personnel overseas is called Serving Abroad for Families and Employees (SAFE). The program consists of two courses: Security Overseas Seminar and Introduction to Working in an Embassy, which can be taken consecutively or separately.

Highly Recommended Pre-assignment Training:

- Personnel assigned to HTHR posts are highly recommended to complete the Diplomacy at High Threat Posts course.
- Personnel assigned to Pakistan are highly recommended to complete Pakistan Familiarization.
- Crisis Leadership is highly recommended for mid-career and above to prepare personnel to lead teams to confront threatening situations overseas.

Additionally, there are a number of elective courses that range from specialized tradecraft skills, Political Military Affairs, Multilateral Affairs, Area Studies, resilience and crisis preparation. Mandatory Training During Assignments:

- Overseas Crisis Management Exercise is a mandatory post-specific tabletop exercise designed for a post's Emergency Action Committee (EAC). Post completes this course every 24 to 30 months (and annually at one-year tour of duty posts).
- Overseas Crisis Management Overview is a mandatory training done in conjunction with the above exercise at Post. This training is made available to all employees at Post, including Locally Employed Staff. Post completes this course every 24 to 30 months (and annually at one-year tour of duty posts).

Mandatory Training Following Assignments:

- The High Stress Assignment Outbriefing Program is mandated for personnel returning from assignments in Iraq, Pakistan, Yemen, Libya, Afghanistan, South Sudan or Central African Republic and highly recommended for others serving at HTHR posts.

**Questions for the Record Submitted to
Deputy Secretary of State Antony J. Blinken by
Representative Matt Salmon
House Foreign Affairs Committee
April 28, 2016**

Question:

Our alliances with Japan and South Korea are the cornerstones of peace and security in Northeast Asia. In response to North Koreans ongoing provocations, I recently introduced H.Res. 634, which urges increased trilateral cooperation among the United States, Japan, and South Korea. This is especially important as we look to counter North Korea's threat. How are we working to increase trilateral cooperation in Northeast Asia, especially with respect to North Korea? What more can we do, and how can we urge our two allies to strengthen this critical partnership?

Answer:

A strong U.S. trilateral partnership with Japan and the Republic of Korea (ROK) is a top strategic priority for the United States. Our three countries are united by strategic interests and shared values. Our strengthened cooperation with the Republic of Korea and Japan over the past year is a testament to the seriousness of our efforts to deepen our cooperation on shared security interests, especially the North Korean threat. We have worked trilaterally to increase pressure on North Korea, counter North Korea's proliferation activities, and focus international attention on North Korea's human rights violations.

Beyond security cooperation, we have also sought ways to broaden our collaboration on other global and regional issues to achieve a multi-faceted and meaningful trilateral partnership. Our health experts have consulted on ways to coordinate more closely in promoting global health security. We will convene our first Middle East dialogue to discuss common approaches to key issues in the region. We are exploring additional frontiers of cooperation: empowering women and girls, countering cyber threats, engaging our peoples directly through public diplomacy. All of these activities represent the new normal – a vibrant trilateral partnership that seeks out new possibilities and areas for cooperation.

For the future, we need to continue our active engagement with both the ROK and Japan. Earlier in April, I participated in the third vice-ministerial level trilateral meeting in Seoul. We have held these meetings on a quarterly basis to provide regular, frequent communication among our three countries, and they are an investment in our shared futures. It is critical that we sustain this level of engagement to also provide a unified and singular message in the face of North Korea's provocative actions.

Just as important, we need to continue to support the ROK's and Japan's efforts to strengthen their bilateral relationship. We are encouraged by the progress they have made and take seriously our role to facilitate this process. We are convinced that both governments are sincere in their efforts to improve their relations and that broadening our collaboration will help to build further goodwill and understanding.

Question:

National Security Advisor Susan Rice recently announced a proposed expansion of the President's Malaria Initiative in an effort to eliminate malaria from Cambodia entirely. How will Malaria elimination in Cambodia help address artemisinin resistance in the broader Mekong Delta sub-region?

Answer:

Eliminating malaria in Cambodia will help address artemisinin resistance in the Greater Mekong Subregion (GMS). In February, Secretary Rice announced the Administration's plans for programming a $200 million increase requested for malaria as part of the Administration's FY 2017 budget request. These plans include expanding malaria efforts in Cambodia to accelerate progress toward malaria elimination, aligned with the Cambodia National Malaria Control program's stated goal of achieving malaria elimination by 2025. The Administration's proposal responds to a call by the global malaria community to eliminate malaria in GMS to directly address the threat of artemisinin resistance. The President's Malaria Initiative (PMI) believes that prioritizing the push toward elimination in Cambodia will produce experience to be applied to elimination efforts across the GMS, with the goal of elimination of malaria in all countries in the region no later than 2030. Ultimately eliminating artemisinin resistance from the region will remove the threat that presently exists of resistance spreading from the GMS countries to other parts of the world.

Artemisinin-based combination therapies are the first-line treatment for malaria in almost all malaria-affected countries worldwide. Resistance to artemisinin was first identified in Cambodia in an area bordering Thailand almost a decade ago, and has since been identified in other countries of the GMS, including Burma, Cambodia, China (Yunnan Province), Lao PDR, Thailand, and Vietnam. The identification of resistance in countries of the GMS has raised fears among the global malaria community that artemisinin resistance could spread beyond the GMS into higher burden malaria areas, particularly sub-Saharan Africa. In the 1960s and 1970s, resistance to chloroquine, the first-line malaria treatment at the time, arose also in the Thai-Cambodian border region and subsequently spread globally. Chloroquine resistance is considered one of the key factors that led to the failure of malaria eradication efforts during that era and also resulted in a significant resurgence of malaria cases and deaths in sub-Saharan Africa during the latter part of the 20th century. Therefore, addressing artemisinin drug resistance in GMS is imperative and the only solution to prevent the spread of artemisinin resistance to other parts of the world.

This call for elimination is bolstered by the significant progress that has been made in GMS countries to reduce malaria transmission by effective malaria programming, including distribution of insecticide-treated bed nets and rapid diagnosis and treatment of malaria cases. Cambodia, for example, through support from PMI and other partners, has experienced significant progress in reducing malaria. Malaria cases have steadily reduced to only approximately 35,000 cases reported in 2015, with only 10 recorded deaths. One district prioritized by PMI for elimination, Sampov Loun in the border region with Thailand, has reported a steady reduction in cases over time, with only 250 cases reported last year, of which only 50 were acquired locally. This translates into less than two percent of the district population now infected with malaria. Such evidence provides support that Cambodia's goal of eliminating malaria by 2025 is achievable, if sufficient resources and effort are focused on elimination program implementation. With additional U.S. government resources, PMI will expand the number of districts where intensified malaria elimination efforts can be supported, resulting in an acceleration of progress toward achieving overall elimination in Cambodia. PMI's efforts in Thailand and Burma also continue to focus on driving down malaria transmission toward elimination, and lessons from the prioritized elimination push in Cambodia will be applied to efforts in Thailand, Burma and more broadly in the Mekong region.